Let's Cook Japanese Food!

Let's Cook Japanese Food!
Everyday Recipes for Home Cooking

By Amy Kaneko

Photographs by Deborah Ory

CHRONICLE BOOKS

SAN FRANCISCO

Library of Congress Cataloging-in-Publication data available.

ISBN-10: 0-8118-4832-9
ISBN-13: 978-0-8118-4832-9

Manufactured in China

Designed by Omnivore: Alice Chung and Karen Hsu
Food and prop styling by Laura L. Hamblen

Distributed in Canada by Raincoast Books
9050 Shaughnessy Street
Vancouver, British Columbia V6P 6E5

10 9 8 7 6 5 4 3 2 1

Chronicle Books LLC
680 Second Street
San Francisco, California 94107

www.chroniclebooks.com

Table of Contents

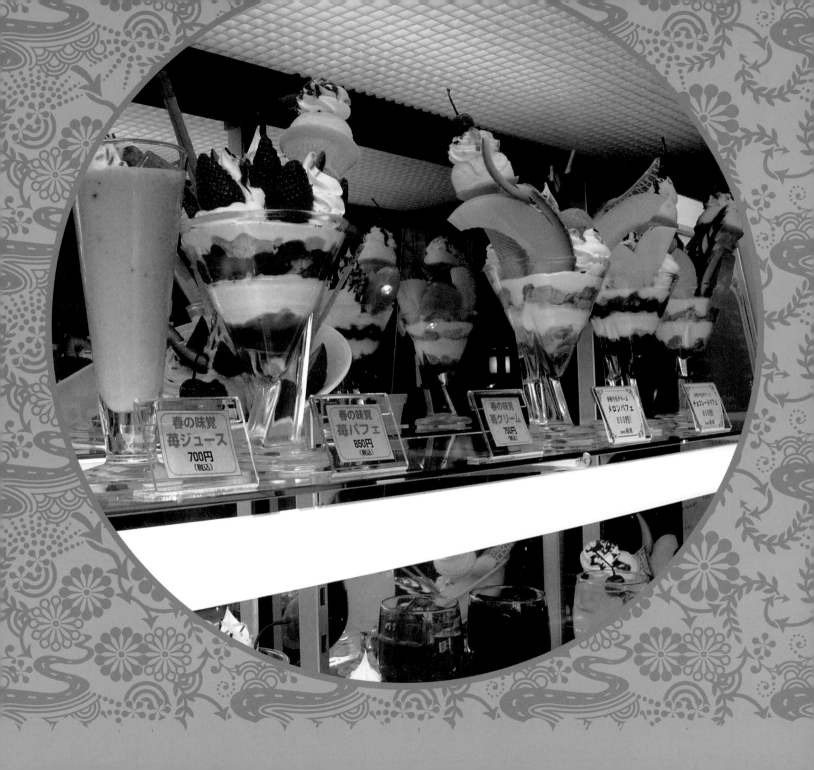

Introduction

I had never eaten sushi until I was eighteen years old. Ten years later, I married it. After an average upbringing in an average suburban town, I met and married Shohei Kaneko. At the time we met, he had lived in the West for only a short time, and when we wed, I discovered that I was marrying into a cultural lexicon about which I knew nothing.

The Japanese language was initially impenetrable, but I knew that I could start learning about the food right away. Early in our marriage we moved to Japan, where I was immediately exposed to Japanese home cooking, a whole new culinary world that I had to start participating in—and fast.

First, I had to learn the rituals. In my mother-in-law's kitchen, an apron was tied around my waist immediately and kitchen slippers were slid onto my feet—never mind that my heels hung over the backs by several inches. Luckily, I love food and I am almost never put off by a challenge, so I wanted to jump in and start cooking with my mother-in-law at once.

She was skeptical about my ability to interpret her directions as we set about assembling our first meal together, and perhaps rightly so. It was to be led off by her version of the soul-warming home-style soup known as kenchin jiru, which in the Kaneko household is a savory mix of tender vegetables, sliced pork, and soft tofu. I soon discovered that it was particularly important that I learn this dish well because it is my husband's favorite. Apparently all I could be trusted to do was cut up the green onions and chop a

few of the vegetables—and then only with a lot of direction. But the soup was delicious, and although my pieces of potato were too small and melted away in the broth, my first attempt at trying to cook Japanese food was praised.

I also sliced up some cucumbers for a simple sunomono (vinegared salad), while my mother-in-law mixed the dressing without looking at a recipe. Then I helped serve each diner some rice, doled out the soup in individual bowls, and put the large plate of cucumber salad on the table, for serving family style. Each diner also had a small plate for all the little okazu (side dishes) that my mother-in-law always serves: the pickled turnips that she makes in large batches a couple of times a year and keeps stored in a hatch under the kitchen floor, the sweet egg omelet left over from an earlier meal, and the spicy codfish roe that Shohei had brought as a present from Tokyo. Once everything was on the table, I was asked to fetch the beer from the outdoor shed (where it's as cold as a refrigerator and where root vegetables are also kept), and we were ready to eat.

Every day at every meal at my mother-in-law's house we were served many little dishes to accompany the main course. There would be a soup, little salads, boiled beans, pickled vegetables, and small bowls of leftovers that had been artfully repurposed. The mottai nai (don't waste) concept is firmly entrenched in Japan, especially with older Japanese, and because my mother-in-law doesn't want to spend too much time getting her meals together, she relies on simplicity and her considerable creativity. Never having seen this type of food in Japanese restaurants in the United States whet my appetite for learning more about home-style Japanese food and how to make it myself. Shohei and I were living in Tokyo when we first arrived, so I had plenty of opportunity to explore the world of everyday Japanese cuisine, at home, at casual restaurants, and at street stands and markets. If we ate something I liked, I would try to learn the recipe and cook it myself. Of course, I got plenty of help from my in-laws, from television cooking shows, and from the numerous Japanese weekly magazines geared to housewives.

During my time in Japan, I noticed how my mother-in-law and sisters-in-law skillfully carried on the honorable tradition of caring for the home and family. They were a model for me, a "career woman" whose Western upbringing didn't have half the traditions of the Japanese household. They taught me the essential cooking and preparation skills for the busy housewife, things that I could easily translate to my life back home in San Francisco. I began with small tasks, like chopping onions or grating daikon for a dish, but I soon graduated to joining them on shopping excursions, where the plan for the evening's meal was often made on the spot, based on what looked good in the market that day.

I was surprised that sushi and tempura, the Japanese dishes that most Westerners have heard of, were rarely part of the menu. Instead, hearty soups, rice dishes, meat, grilled fish, and quick stir-fries were the focus. Some of the elements were unfamiliar, but it seemed as if the sauces and marinades were usually made from the same basic ingredients, the preparations were relatively simple, and the service, rather than an elaborate ceremony, was mostly family style. When all of the Kanekos are in attendance, there are sixteen people around the dinner table, so this approach seemed to be the most efficient. I also observed that there was no shame in serving a combination of homemade and purchased foods. For example, my mother-in-law would make fried rice and miso soup and serve them with purchased croquettes from a nearby take-out shop, bottled croquette sauce from the grocery store, and a dish of boiled octopus that she picked up at the local deli.

Some of the dishes that I liked best were those that appealed to my Western tastes—and were, in fact, Japanese versions of Western dishes, such as the French-inspired croquettes. Japanese cooks began introducing these adaptations in the early 1900s, and the new tastes were enthusiastically embraced. (Japanese-style Chinese food, including ramen noodles and gyoza [dumplings], became popular at about the same time.) This culinary tradition, known as yoshoku, or Western food, was ubiquitous on the table of one of my sisters-in-law and in casual restaurants in cities and towns all over Japan, and it quickly became a favorite of mine.

Yoshoku dishes, which are most commonly adopted from French (particularly popular), Italian, and even American cuisine, are Western in both presentation and many ingredients, which made them perfect for me to try to make at home. I found the idea of mastering these recipes much less intimidating than attempting

to duplicate the beautiful washoku, or traditional Japanese food, that I had thought encompassed all of Japanese cuisine. They were a more accessible path to the everyday cuisine of my new home—a path with a less-steep learning curve.

Chuka ryori became my other favorite for cooking at home, as it is for so many Japanese home cooks. Borrowing from traditional Chinese dishes, mostly stir fries and quick-cooking meat and vegetable recipes, chuka ryori is commonly found at lunch counters, in the deparchika (the basement "food fair" in many department stores), and at home. Mapo Dofu, Kanitama, Ebi no Chiri So-su, and Chahan are just a few examples of chuka ryori that have worked their way into the modern Japanese repertoire. My husband is a particular fan of chuka ryori, so I made sure to add some of these terrific recipes to my repertoire as well!

But where was dessert? Imagine my surprise and (I have to admit) dismay when my new Japanese husband expressed exactly zero interest in perpetuating my lifelong dessert tradition in our new home. The reason was simple: Japanese do not end their meals with a sweet. I was happy to learn that while I might not get dessert after dinner, Japanese cuisine still has a lot of sweets. The afternoon tea break is when cakes and other desserts are eaten, and at my mother-in-law's house, we would sit down at teatime to a purchased castella (a type of sponge cake, borrowed from the Iberian Peninsula), some bean paste sweets, a sweet red bean "soup" (shiruko), or a plate of sliced Nagano apples, arguably Japan's best.

With this introduction to Japanese home cooking, I put my mind to learning how to cook the dishes that I liked and that my husband had grown up eating. Knowing we were going to move back to the States, I wanted to use my time well to develop a good repertoire of recipes to take back with me. Luckily, Japan is a paradise for food lovers, with food being sold seemingly everywhere. Convenience stores offer a terrific assortment of hot lunches, stuffed and grilled rice balls, sandwiches, and otsumami (small dishes). There are kiosks selling roasted chestnuts or other snacks; yatai (street stands) offering ramen noodle soup, okonomiyaki, yaki-soba, and more; and deparchika featuring dozens of individual "shops," each with a different specialty, from tempura to Korean kimchee, sushi to potato croquettes.

I sampled it all. I read Japanese cookbooks and magazines and bugged my mother-in-law and sisters-in-law for recipes. I tested my creations incessantly on my sometimes enthusiastic, sometimes merely tolerant, sometimes downright ornery, taster, Shohei. And I finally developed a selection of recipes that I could cook no matter what, and that we actually liked to eat. I began to feel a little bit like a competent Japanese housewife myself (except that I still resisted wearing the apron).

Then we moved back to San Francisco. At first I had a hard time trying to continue to cook Japanese food here. Some of the recipes I had learned called for ingredients that are not easy to find outside of Japan. But when I tried numerous restaurants in

ビーフステーキ
ロコモコ

¥680
(税込714)

テリヤキハンバーグ
ロコモコ

¥690
(税込725)

San Francisco and New York, looking for the food I missed, I was disappointed that so few of the dishes that I had enjoyed in Japan had made their way here, and the ones that had didn't taste like the real thing.

So I started to cook Japanese food again—the everyday food that people in Japan eat in coffee shops, casual restaurants, and around the family dinner table. I am lucky to live in San Francisco and have access to a number of Japanese markets. But when my mother and my friends who live in other parts of the country would call me for my recipes, I would have to adapt my favorites for them because they could not always find some of the ingredients near their homes.

When I began putting together this book, I decided to include only the recipes that are the most familiar to me and that I either learned from my Japanese family or have managed to re-create successfully in my own kitchen after first eating them in coffee shops or restaurants in Japan. Many classic Japanese dishes are included, but some others are not for a trio of reasons: I don't have enough familiarity with them, my family is not that fond of them, or the ingredients for making them properly are not easily available. I have stayed as true to the authentic taste of Japan in the recipes as possible, substituting Western ingredients or methods only when ease of preparation demands it. Simply put, these recipes rely on easy-to-master cooking techniques and ingredients that can be found in most well-stocked Western supermarkets. And while the dishes can look very appealing, you

should not feel that you must conform to the rules of traditional Japanese presentation. If you prefer to spoon a dish on top of a mound of rice, rather than alongside it, feel free to do so.

Also, don't worry that you will need to cook an all-Japanese meal to enjoy these recipes. Japanese try to eat thirty different types of food every day, a wide variety that ensures that they consume all the necessary nutrients, and the time-honored Japanese meal includes a steamed dish, a simmered dish, a soup, a fried dish, and a grilled dish, as well as pickles and rice. Both of those traditions were too demanding for me in my busy life, so I adapted a more easygoing "mix and match" attitude. I have divided the recipes into chapters by their main ingredient, rather than by course or by cooking technique, making it easy to find the foods you like best. You can put together a Japanese meal of your own design (many of the recipes include tips for assembling menus), or you can slip one or two recipes onto your Western menus, to create an appealing blend of East and West that echoes the style of Japanese home cooking today.

With this book, you will soon be cooking what Japanese people eat every day—dishes that are quick, easy, and, of course, delicious. Itadakimasu! (Let's eat!)

—Amy Kaneko

Ingredients and Equipment

I have taken care to create the authentic flavor of home-style Japanese recipes using ingredients available in regular markets, so that you won't have to change your usual shopping routine. This may initially surprise you, given what you have enjoyed in Japanese restaurants. But you will soon discover that many of the dishes that you have eaten are simply interesting uses of familiar foods, rather than mixtures of exotic ingredients. If you have trouble finding any of the ingredients, check the Sources section (page 162) for online possibilities.

Equipment needs are equally undemanding. When I returned to a Western-style kitchen in the United States after living in Japan, I found that I needed very few new tools to keep cooking the recipes I had mastered in Tokyo. A few pieces of specialized equipment, such as a rice cooker and a mandoline, make some of the common tasks of Japanese cooking a little easier, but most tasks can be accomplished with the same everyday equipment you use for cooking Western meals.

O-ryori ganbatte ne!
(Good luck and try hard to cook Japanese food!)

Ingredients

BAMBOO SHOOTS
Crunchy young bamboo shoots, called *takenoko*, are prized in Japan. Their first appearance in the market each year heralds the beginning of spring, and during those days you will find fresh bamboo shoots on restaurant menus. They are typically prepared simply, usually chilled and napped with a lemony dressing. Fresh bamboo shoots are not readily available outside of Japan, nor are they part of everyday cuisine even inside Japan. Instead, cooks use boiled bamboo shoots, which are sold canned or in plastic packs. Here, they are usually sold whole (cone-shaped shoots) or sliced. Rinse under running cold water before using.

BENI SHOGA
See Ginger.

CABBAGE
Regular green head cabbage, or *cabegi*, is used in many modern Japanese dishes. To use, remove and discard the outer layer of leaves and cut as directed in individual recipes. When a recipe calls for shredded cabbage (the traditional accompaniment to *tonkatsu* and other fried dishes), use a mandoline, a food processor, or a sharp knife and lots of patience to shred it, and then put it in a large bowl filled with ice water and slip the bowl into the refrigerator for about 30 minutes to crisp. I am lucky that my local market sells prewashed and finely shredded cabbage for coleslaw in plastic bags. After crisping it up in ice water, it is as good as freshly cut cabbage—and much less time-consuming to prepare! *See also* Napa cabbage.

CHILI BEAN PASTE
See Sauces.

CORNSTARCH
Katakuriko, originally made from the root of the dogtooth violet and now made from the considerably less exotic Irish potato, is the most commonly used thickener for cooked sauces. The switch to the Irish potato has made *katakuriko* far less costly to manufacture and allows it to be translated as simply potato starch. Cornstarch, which is more widely available, is a good substitute and I have used it in my recipes. It is mixed with water in varying ratios, depending on the dish, and then added near the end of cooking. Always stir the mixture again briefly just before using (it separates upon standing) and add it slowly, stirring it into the dish until the desired consistency is achieved. Cornstarch is also a good coating for meat or chicken

for deep-frying (see *Toriniku Kara-age*, page 110), yielding crispy results.

CUCUMBER

The cucumber, or *kyuri*, grown in Japan and generally not found outside Japanese markets in the United States, is small and has dense flesh,

thin skin, and few seeds. You can use English, or hothouse, cucumbers in its place. You can leave the skin on English cucumbers (it is rarely waxed, unlike the skin of outdoor varieties, which are typically waxed to lengthen shelf life), but I peel it away, partially for an attractive look.

To prepare the peeled cucumbers for recipes in this book, cut them in half lengthwise, scoop out any seeds with the tip of a spoon, and slice the halves crosswise to create half-moons. (Because Japanese cucumbers are slimmer, they are not halved; they are instead simply cut into rounds.) Place the slices in a colander, salt them, and leave them to stand for about 30 minutes to drain away excess water. Finally, give the drained slices a good squeeze to make them as dry as you can before using in salads, cold noodles, or other dishes.

DAIKON

This large (10 to 20 inches long), creamy white, fat, crisp radish is a common ingredient in all types of Japanese dishes. It is eaten raw, pickled, and simmered in soups and braises. While these giant radishes are readily found in all types of Asian markets, they are not often stocked in regular groceries, unless the store is in an area with a large Asian community.

Choose firm radishes with smooth, unwrinkled skin and a distinctive, though not overly strong, smell. To use, peel and then cut as directed in individual recipes. Grated daikon is used in dipping sauces for tempura and other fried foods (it is believed to aid in digestion) and noodles and is served with certain types of grilled fish. To grate, use any fine-rasp grater or an *oroshi* (see page 22). Grated daikon releases a lot of water, which you must squeeze out by hand before serving. More readily available, red radishes have a sharper flavor than daikon, but they can be peeled and used as a substitute for daikon in the recipes in this book. You can grate them in a food processor but be careful not to overprocess.

DASHI

At the heart of many Japanese recipes, dashi is stock made from dried bonito flakes or dried anchovies or sardines. In spite of how this description sounds, the stock does not have a strong fishy taste. Many types of dashi exist, but for the most part, the modern Japanese home cook uses *dashi-no-moto*, instant dashi in powder, granule, or teabag form.

Dashi-no-moto is available in Asian markets and by mail order, but you can also buy it at many Western markets. You can also use instant granules marketed under the name *hondashi*, which is usually a soup base made from bonito flakes and *konbu*, a type of kelp, but some-times also contains broth from dried shiitake mushrooms, ground tiny anchovies, and/or other seasonings.

I recommend that you use any basic *katsuo* (bonito) dashi, with or without monosodium glutamate as you like (check the label to see if it is included). All types of instant dashi keep well—like chicken bouillon—and only a small amount is used for each recipe, so if you cannot pick it up easily at a local store, mail order a big supply to have on hand. It is essential for making authentic-tasting miso soup and many other recipes, and is the one "Japanese" ingredient that I encourage you to seek out. I have tried to substitute chicken broth for dashi in as many recipes as possible. In the ones in which dashi still appears, you can use reduced-fat, low-sodium canned chicken or vegetable broth in its place, but the results will not be as authentic.

EDAMAME

These green soybeans in fuzzy green pods are a popular snack food, especially as an accompaniment to

beer or sake. Eat the beans only, of course, by forcing them from the pod with your lips directly into your mouth. They are available frozen in bags in the shell and shelled in Japanese markets and some Western markets, and more rarely fresh in the shell, the pods still attached to their stalks, in Japanese markets and some farmers' markets. Although I don't call for them in any recipe, *edamame* are easy to prepare (cook the frozen ones according to package directions, and boil the fresh ones in generously salted boiling water for about 10 minutes), making them a quick way to add a Japanese snack to your repertoire.

EGGPLANT

There are a lot of recipes that call for eggplant, or *nasu*, in this book because many modern dishes use it—and also because my husband and children—and I, too—love eating it. The best type to use is the long, slender, deep purple Japanese eggplant, although long, lavender Chinese eggplants are fine, too. Both have denser flesh and far fewer seeds than larger varieties.

Choose firm, unblemished eggplants with no discoloration or soft spots. If you must use a large globe eggplant, slice it into disks or into "sticks," and then discard the section with the most seeds, which make most dishes look dark and unappealing and adversely affect the texture. Recipes often call for frying the eggplant in oil first by itself and then cooking it in a sauce. This creates a soft texture and rich taste. It is best not to fry eggplants straight from the refrigerator. Cold eggplant soaks up more oil than room-temperature eggplants.

GINGER

Fresh ginger, or *shoga*, is easily found in most supermarkets. Look for

smooth, creamy yellow or tan skin. Most of my recipes call for grated ginger or ginger juice. Grated or minced ginger is sometimes available in convenient jars, which must be stored in the refrigerator after opening.

To grate your own ginger, peel away the thin skin with a paring knife or vegetable peeler and then run the flesh across the fine rasps of a grater, either a Japanese *oroshi* (see page 22) or a handheld Western grater. Always cut a piece about an inch longer than you need to avoid nicking your fingers on the sharp rasps. Grating ginger can be a chore, but you usually need only a small amount, so it is over fairly quickly.

To extract ginger juice, you don't need to peel the ginger. Simply grate it and then squeeze the pulp in your hand to release the juice. A 3½-inch piece of fresh ginger yields about 2 teaspoons juice. When making soups with meat, a Japanese cook often slips a large slice of unpeeled ginger into the broth to reduce the "meaty" smell that would otherwise fill the typically small Japanese kitchen.

Beni shoga: Bright pink, sharp-flavored, vinegary matchsticks of marinated ginger, this is sometimes stocked in the refrigerated Asian section of Western markets (with the

dumpling wrappers and tofu). It is used in small amounts—no more than a teaspoon or two—to garnish *Hiyashi Chuka* (page 146), *Yakisoba* (page 152), and the Hakata- and Tonkotsu-style ramen popular on the island of Kyushu. Both boast a particularly rich broth based on pork bones, and the vinegary ginger provides a nice contrast to the richness. *Beni shoga* is also sometimes mixed into *okonomiyaki* (page 34) and *takoyaki* (page 36) batter. Do not mistake *beni shoga* for *gari*, the pale marinated ginger served with sushi.

GOMA DARE
See Sauces.

GREEN ONION
Green onions, or *negi*, are used extensively in Japanese cooking. Though similar in flavor to the green onion found in Western markets, the Japanese *negi* is closer in size to a thin leek. Western green onions are a perfect substitute—I have used them for the recipes in this book—though you need 4 or 5 of them for every large *negi*. In most cases, you will use

the white and all but the very top of the green parts. Usually I wash the onion, peel off and discard the outer layer, slice the onion in half lengthwise, and then mince or thinly slice. For some recipes, such as the *Sukiyaki* on page 134, the onions are cut on the diagonal into 2-inch lengths.

HOT CHILI OIL
See Oils.

ICHIMI TOGARASHI
See Shichimi togarashi and *Ichimi togarashi*.

KABOCHA PUMPKIN
This round, heavy gourd, known as both a pumpkin and a squash, has green-and-white mottled skin, dense orange flesh, and a sweet full flavor. Because the skin is very hard, you will need to use a large, heavy knife to cut the squash into chunks. The skin is completely edible when cooked, however, and so recipes call for removing the stem and seeds, but most of them don't call for peeling the pumpkin. If you cannot find *kabocha* (I have found it as part of the decorative seasonal

gourd display at my regular market), butternut squash is an acceptable substitute for many dishes. It must be peeled, however, and does not have the same delectable floury yet moist texture.

KARASHI
Japanese brands of Chinese-style hot yellow mustard powder, or *karashi*, are hard to find outside of Asian markets, but Chinese brands, which are more common, will do. This condiment is served in a little dab for mixing with *tonkatsu* sauce for accompanying *tonkatsu* or other fried dishes, and for mixing with the sauce for *Hiyashi Chuka* (page 146). It's pretty hot, so taste it before you start mixing it in. Most brands are mixed in a ratio of 2 teaspoons mustard powder to 1 tablespoon water. Check the package for directions.

MAYONNAISE
Mayonnaise is mixed with other ingredients in some recipes in this book, including the *korokke* (croquettes) made with pumpkin on page 52 and the crispy meat patties on page 128. When used in this way, you don't get the taste of mayonnaise, but rather the richness and a kind of juiciness. However, Japanese do love to use mayonnaise in salads and as a condiment. Japanese mayonnaise has a particular flavor, more acidic than the eggy richness of its European or Western counterparts. You can either buy Japanese mayonnaise online (I like Kewpie brand; my husband always brings home several squeeze bottles from his trips to Japan), or use regular mayonnaise with a little rice vinegar or fresh lemon juice added to taste, being careful not to thin it too much.

MEATS
I have included many modern, Western-inspired recipes in this book that use a good deal more meat than you might expect for Japanese food. Meat is, of course, widely available and regularly used in Japanese cooking today, but because it typically is only one element, rather than the focus, of a dish, it is often ground or very thinly sliced.

Some of my chicken recipes call for ground chicken. I use dark meat only, as it contributes good flavor and succulence, while I find the white meat delivers neither. Sometimes it is difficult to find ground chicken, but Asian markets almost always have it as a mixture of dark and white meat, which works well in all the recipes here that call for this ingredient. You can grind your own in a food processor, using

boneless, skinless thighs (or ask your butcher to do it), or you can substitute ground turkey. I find the turkey too lean, but the taste is similar, so it will do in a pinch. For other recipes, I have specified boneless, skinless chicken thigh meat. I rarely use chicken breast, except when I make *Chikin Katsu* (page 102). The dark thigh meat has far better flavor and also will be juicier because it has some fat in it. Chicken breast cooks too fast, becomes tough, and doesn't deliver enough flavor, though it can work as an addition to a bowl of soba noodle soup (page 150).

I also use a lot of ground pork in my recipes. It is rich tasting and juicy, lends itself well to some of the spicier dishes, and provides an extra flavor element when mixed with ground beef. A friend who was making one of my recipes that called for ground pork decided to substitute plain pork sausages, removed from their casing, when he discovered his market didn't carry ground pork. It was quick thinking, but the taste and texture of

sausage are different from ground pork, so sausages are not a good substitute. If you can't find ground pork—remember, you can ask your butcher to grind it for you—then grind your own in a food processor, using pork tenderloin or pork loin.

In addition, many of the soups and stir-fries call for a tender, fatty pork cut known as *baraniku*, literally "belly meat." This is not easy to find outside of Japan except in Japanese, Korean, or Chinese markets. As an alternative, I have used thick-cut bacon in many recipes. Depending on how lean your bacon is, you may need to render some of the fat before you use the bacon in a recipe, as it can be fattier than *baraniku* would be. You can also use boneless pork shoulder. Freeze it partially, leaving it for an hour or so, and use a sharp knife and some muscle power to slice—almost shave it—thinly.

Japanese cattle, grain-fed, massaged beer drinkers that they are, produce some of the most delectable, deli-

cately rich, beefy-tasting meat in the world. I am not cooking with that. Neither are you. When I call for beef, or *gyuniku*, I typically want you to use rib eye or sirloin. It is usually sliced paper-thin, which is something most butchers probably won't do for you unless they are both very nice and very patient. To do it at home, cut the steak into two pieces (in these smaller chunks, it will freeze faster and the middle will be firm, rather than soft) and put them in the freezer for an hour, or until they are almost frozen. Then, with a good sharp knife, you will be able to slice—again, almost shave—the beef the way it needs to be cut for several of the recipes in this book, such as *Hayashi Raisu* (page 124) and *Gyudon* (page 120). Ground beef (not the leanest) is used for dishes like *Menchi Katsu* (page 128).

MIRIN

This sweetened rice wine (sweet cooking sake), an integral element in Japanese flavoring, is readily available. It imparts sweetness and good glazing properties to teriyaki sauce, is frequently added to simmered dishes, and is often used in place of sugar because it contributes a more complex sweetness. Sauces that include mirin are heated before using to cook off the alcohol taste and concentrate the flavor. I use a regular mirin made by Takara that has an alcohol content of about 12 percent.

Other types of mirin include naturally brewed *hon mirin*, or "true mirin," which has a slightly higher alcohol content, and *aji mirin*, which is seasoned with corn syrup and salt and which I

don't recommend. Regular mirin or *hon mirin* will work well in all of the recipes in this book with no discernable difference in flavor.

MISO

While Shohei won't tolerate chicken for lunch one day and then for dinner the next, he is perfectly happy to drink miso soup at every meal. Japanese are passionate about this national food. There are many, many different types, but basically miso is a paste made from fermented soybeans, salt, rice or barley, and a starter culture. If you can find different types (often named after the town where they were first made), the best thing to do is to try them to decide which type tastes best to you. Miso ranges from very light yellow, known as *shiro-miso* (*shiro* means "white") or Saikyo miso, to a

deep, rich brick-red brown, known as *aka-miso* (*aka* means "red"), with many variations in between. My family likes golden yellow Shinshu miso (named after my husband's home region). Most people just starting to eat miso favor *shiro-miso*, which is mild and almost sweet and is also the type most widely available outside of Asian markets. Although miso is high in sodium, it contains a lot of protein and nutrients and is considered a health food.

NAPA CABBAGE

This elongated, pale green, ruffly leaved cabbage, known as *hakusai* in Japanese and sometimes called Chinese cabbage, has a milder taste than the round green cabbage commonly used in Western cuisine. Cooks remove any damaged outer leaves and then usually chop the cabbage

for adding to stir-fries, *gyoza* fillings, simmered dishes, or soups. The Japanese never eat napa cabbage raw, though it is a popular vegetable for pickling. You usually will not need more than half the head for any recipe in this book. Wrap the unused portion in plastic wrap and store in the refrigerator for up to 4 days. If it is brown or soggy, it's over the hill. Sometimes when the outer leaves look bad, you can peel them away and still have some salvageable *hakusai*. I can usually find napa cabbage at my regular market, but if you can't find it, use green head cabbage (*see* Cabbage).

NOODLES

Noodles are a daily food in Japan. There is a huge variety, only some of which you will be able to find in your local market. Even though it sounds terrible, for some of my recipes, you can use the noodles in an instant-ramen package (not the cup style) and just discard the flavor packet. Don't overcook them, as they have a tendency to become mushy. I have even used spaghetti in some recipes because the noodles normally used in the dish are not easily found in the States. Don't worry. Even with such

substitutions, the recipes still taste good. Japanese soba, *udon*, and ramen are all easily found outside of Japan.

There is no substitute for light brown soba noodles, made from a mix of buckwheat and wheat flours, especially when making *zaru soba* (page 150). They have a nutty flavor and a firm texture and taste best when cooked al dente. They are also served hot in broth (page 150).

Popular at Japanese restaurants outside of Japan, thick, white *udon* noodles, made from wheat flour, are used in soups; are added to hearty one-pot dishes such as *nabeyaki udon*, a rich, hot soup-stew with chicken, shrimp tempura, and vegetables; and are sometimes eaten cold with a dipping sauce. The same dough in different thicknesses is used to make *somen* (thinner noodles) and *kishi-men* (flat noodles), both of which are usually eaten cold.

Best known as a quick, cheap dinner for college students and others, instant ramen has taken the world by storm. The thin, yellow wheat noodles are served in broth and stir-fried. You can also eat them cold in *Hiyashi Chuka* (page 146), substituting ramen noodles for the spaghetti, though I think that the spaghetti yields a better taste and texture.

NORI

Nori (also known as laver, a type of seaweed) is sold as plain pressed sheets and also toasted sheets, the latter known as *yakinori*. The thin sheets of dark green—almost black—dried seaweed come in various grades and shapes, from squares to shreds to rectangles that are perfectly sized for wrapping around a rice ball (see *Onigiri*, page 142). As long as nori is crisp, it will work for most recipes. It comes wrapped in cellophane packages that often contain a small

packet of silicone pellets, placed there to absorb any moisture—the enemy of crisp nori. A delicious

snack food (my kids like a "nori sandwich" with Cheddar cheese), nori is used for sushi, crumbled over rice, and shredded over cold noodle dishes, hot noodle soups, and even spaghetti.

Aonori (literally "blue" nori), a different type of seaweed, is sold dried and already crushed into small flakes, usually in a packet or a shaker. It has a very fresh marine aroma and, despite the translation, is a medium green. It is sprinkled on dishes such as *Okonomiyaki* (page 34).

OILS

In most recipes, I have specified canola oil or other neutral vegetable oil. By *neutral* I mean bland, so you might use safflower, corn, or another oil that has little or no flavor. I use canola oil for stir-frying and deep-frying because it gets nice and hot without smoking, it has no taste, and it has less of the stuff in it that's bad for you.

Sesame oil, or *goma abura*, is used in many Japanese recipes that have been adopted from the Chinese kitchen. It is primarily a seasoning oil, rather than a cooking oil, though some Chinese-style dishes call for frying meat in sesame oil. Rancidity can be a problem, so check the bottle for a sell-by date (not all bottles have them) and buy from markets with a high turnover. Once opened, store sesame oil in a cool, dark, dry place, but try to use it quickly. Look for 100 percent pure sesame oil. I use either of two Japanese brands, Kadoya or Maruhon.

Hot chili oil, or *rayu*, is a popular condiment made by adding chilies to a neutral vegetable oil. It's great for jazzing up Chinese-inspired dishes

like *Ebi no Chiri So-su* (page 76), *Mapo Dofu* (page 28), and ramen soup (page 155). Many regular markets carry chili oil. You might try a few brands to find the flavor you like best. Be sure that the base is a neutral oil and not sesame oil.

OKONOMIYAKI SAUCE

See Sauces.

PANKO

Also called Japanese bread crumbs or honey-wheat bread crumbs, these light-colored, nearly flat "shards" of flaked wheat flour are used for many of the deep-fried recipes in this book, including *Tonkatsu* (page 101), *Ebi Furai* (page 78), and various *korokke* (croquettes). In fact, most fried foods in Japan other than tempura, which uses a batter, are coated with *panko*, which results in a light and very crispy coating. *Panko* is readily available in plastic bags in the Asian or international foods section of regular markets. It is quite inexpensive. I usually keep it, repackaged in a freezer bag, in my freezer, so I always have some on hand.

RAMEN NOODLES

See Noodles.

RICE

I could go on at length about the importance of rice to the Japanese diet and culture, about its history, the customs surrounding it, and the many different types available in Japan. But instead I will simply say that nearly every Japanese home-style meal includes a bowl of rice. In the West, the rice you want is usually labeled Japanese or short grain. Never

buy sweet rice, sometimes called glutinous rice, which is used mainly for *mochi* (rice cakes) and various other confections, or converted white rice, which lacks the proper texture.

Short-grain rice is stickier than long grain, which makes it easier to eat with chopsticks, and it can be found at almost any grocery. Brown rice, which still has the whole bran intact ("polishing" removes all the bran for white rice), is available, though not popular in Japanese home kitchens. Its strong taste and chewy texture interferes with other dishes. When I'm calling my family to the table at dinnertime, I always shout "*Gohan desu yo!*" which means, more or less, "It's rice!" For details on how to cook a good pot of rice, including the need to rinse, rinse, rinse, see page 141.

RICE VINEGAR

Milder than distilled white vinegar or white or red wine vinegar, rice vinegar, called *komezu*, is the most common vinegar used in Japanese cooking. It is available at most markets, so you don't have to think about tracking down a substitute. It is a necessary ingredient in salad dressings and sauces, and you may find that you can integrate its mild acidic taste into your other cooking. Rice vinegar is also used for pickling and for preventing certain foods, such as apples and potatoes, from turning brown due to oxidation. Make sure that you buy unseasoned rice vinegar for the recipes in this book.

My friends Hiroshi and Ikko each drink a tiny cup of *komezu* daily for their health. They believe it makes the blood strong.

SAKE

Sake is for drinking and for cooking. For cooking purposes, any inexpensive brand will do. It can even do for drinking, warmed in your microwave for about a minute. As with fine wines, there is a whole world of fine sake that I am not going to get into here. (Check out my friend Beau Timken's store, True Sake, at www.truesake.com, if you want to learn more.) Just know that for cooking, the most basic sake will be fine. Buy the big bottle. It's inexpensive and keeps well in the pantry (no refrigeration necessary). Sake is one of the key Japanese flavorings, along with soy sauce, mirin, dashi, and sugar.

SAUCES

I don't want you to think that Japanese cooks create all of the sauces for modern Japanese dishes from scratch. In fact, just the opposite is the case. Bottled sauces for the most common dishes are in widespread use, and there is no shame in using them to achieve the right Japanese flavor. Some very simple flavorings are usu- ally made from scratch, such as simmered liquids made from mirin, soy sauce, sugar, and sake, but prepared sauces save the day for Western-style dishes like *Yakisoba* (page 152), *Okonomiyaki* (page 34), *Tonkatsu* (page 101), and *Hamburg* (page 131). Luckily, these dishes are also popular with people outside of Japan, so many regular markets carry the sauces. The most commonly used of these sauces are included here.

Chili Bean Paste: Known as *toban djan*, this dark red paste contains bits of hot red chili, garlic, and mashed soybeans. Strong flavored and spicy, it is frequently used in such Chinese-inspired recipes as *Mapo Dofu* (page 28), *Ebi no Chiri So-su* (page 76), and *Shohci no Butaniku to Goma Ramen* (page 155). It is hot, but not incendiary. Taste it before you use it to determine your own tolerance. Look for chili bean paste stocked alongside other Asian sauces in the international food aisle of most supermarkets. If you can't find it, chili garlic paste or chili garlic sauce can be substituted.

Goma Dare: This bottled sesame sauce, typically a mixture of sesame seeds, soy sauce, sugar, dashi, mirin, and other ingredients, is used straight from the bottle to dress steamed vegetables or as dipping sauce for *nabemono* (one-pot dishes).

Okonomiyaki Sauce: This sweet sour-fruity combination of tomato, fruit, vinegar, and spices is closely related to *tonkatsu* sauce and *yakisoba* sauce, and in a pinch, any one of the three can be substituted for the others. If your regular market carries it, it will be stocked in the international food aisle along with other Asian sauces.

Oyster Sauce: Thick, salty, and slightly briny, this Chinese flavor waker-upper is combined with other sauces or used in small amounts on its own to enhance other flavors. Oyster sauce keeps well in the refrigerator after opening, and if the cap is cleaned and tightly closed after using, it will have a long life. It's found in the Chinese food section or with other Asian sauces in the international food aisle.

Ponzu Sauce: This bottled sauce combines citrus-flavored vinegar with soy sauce. The citrus fruit is traditionally *yuzu*, a type of citron, but versions using lemon, lime, or *sudachi* (a tiny Japanese lime) are also found in Japanese stores. The *ponzu* sauce found in most Western markets is fine for serving with the *Sukiyaki* on page 134, where the refreshing and cleansing bite of the citrus perfectly offsets the fatty richness of the meat. If you don't care for monosodium glutamate, check the label, as many brands include this flavor enhancer. Though nontraditional, *ponzu* can also be used as a seasoning for grilled or fried fish, or in salad dressings for a vinegary, salty kick.

Sukiyaki Sauce: You can purchase this sauce, which is used for cooking the dish, but it can also be made from scratch if you have soy sauce, mirin, and sugar on hand.

Teriyaki Sauce: This is probably the most popular Japanese sauce available outside of Japan. You can buy it in flavored versions, such as garlic. I've used only the regular flavor in my recipes. You can also make this one yourself. It's supereasy (see the recipe for yellowtail on page 86 for a favorite version) and the taste can be adjusted to how you like it.

Tomato Ketchup: The tomatoey secret in many Japanese dishes, Western ketchup, with its slightly sweet tomato taste, is a common ingredient in many of my recipes, either mixed with other ingredients or on its own. Kagome is the largest Japanese brand, but the ketchup tastes just like Heinz.

Tonkatsu Sauce: Also called fruit sauce, this thick, slightly sweet, spiced (think cloves) sauce is indispensable in the modern Japanese kitchen. Bull Dog is a famous Japanese brand, but Kikkoman is the most widely available brand outside of Japan. Almost no one ever makes this sauce at home, so if you can't find it at your market, you can buy it online. It keeps in the refrigerator for a long time after opening.

Tsuyu: This sauce, which doubles as a soup base and a seasoning, is diluted for use as a broth for hot soba and *udon* or as a dipping sauce for soba and tempura. (*Memmi* sauce, a concentrated noodle soup base, is similar.) *Tsuyu* is available from several different manufacturers, with most versions containing dashi, sake, soy sauce, and sometimes mirin or sugar. The difference between the various brands is usually the degree of sweetness. *Tentsuyu*, the classic dipping sauce for tempura, is a fairly concentrated version of *tsuyu*, probably to balance the relatively strong flavor of the fried food. You can use a purchased sauce, diluting it as indicated on the bottle, if you don't want to make the homemade sauce that I have included with the tempura recipe on page 70. I have also included a homemade *tsuyu* sauce, milder than the tempura version, for dipping cold soba (page 149). A mild *tsuyu* is also recommended for *Agedashi Dofu* (page 26), but since you need only a small amount, a diluted bottled product is easiest.

Worcestershire Sauce: This British sauce is a major ingredient in Japan's Western-style recipes. I had never used it much before starting to cook Japanese food, and now I love its vinegary rich flavor. Although thicker in texture, your favorite steak sauce can also work in a recipe calling for Worcestershire sauce. Just a little bit will perk up a dish.

Yakisoba Sauce: Yet another variation on the *tonkatsu*-sauce theme, bottled (or squeeze-bottled) *yakisoba* sauce is the way to go. It has an unmistakable tang and spice that give the stir-fried noodle dish its distinctive flavor. You probably won't find it in your regular market, but you should seek it out online. It makes the dish. While my husband cooks a version of *yakisoba* without sauce—using just soy sauce and pepper—I prefer the real thing, which never fails to evoke memories of Japanese street fairs, where the dish is always sold.

SESAME OIL
See Oils.

SESAME SEEDS
Some people say that it is hard to buy sesame seeds or sesame oil that hasn't already gone rancid. Maybe I am just lucky, but rancidity has never been a problem. Or, maybe it is because I purchase most of my sesame seeds at Asian markets, where there is a high turnover. Regardless of where you buy your sesame seeds, look for airtight packages and refrigerate the seeds in an airtight container after opening. I

use only white sesame seeds because they are easy to get. Black ones have a stronger

sesame taste and are more visually exciting, but all the recipes in this book work fine with white.

You will want to toast your sesame seeds; even if you have purchased seeds labeled roasted, they still need to be toasted to bring out the best flavor. To toast, heat a nonstick frying pan over medium-high heat. When the pan is hot, add the sesame seeds and heat, shaking the pan often to move the seeds around in it, until the seeds are golden and are releasing a heady sesame aroma. This will take only 3 to 4 minutes. Immediately pour the toasted seeds onto a plate, as they can go quickly from nicely toasted to irretrievably burned.

SHICHIMI TOGARASHI AND ICHIMI TOGARASHI
Shichimi means "seven flavors," and *togarashi* means "hot red pepper." *Shichimi togarashi* is a traditional spice mix made up of seven different peppers and other seasonings. Sometimes called seven-spice pow-

der in English and also known as *nanami* in Japanese, it is great sprinkled into soups and on noodles, tempura, fried chicken, and more. Experiment— it's not too spicy but definitely adds a nice little kick. You can find it at well-stocked supermarkets, at Asian groceries, and online. *Ichimi* means "one spice," so *ichimi togarashi* is simply hot red pepper, finely ground. If you like spicy, this is the one for you.

SHIITAKE MUSHROOMS
These mushrooms have been traditionally cultivated on the logs of the

shii tree, hence the name (*take* means "mushroom"). They are meaty, dark brown, and have a strong mushroomy aroma and a smoky taste. Most recipes call for discarding the stems; they are usually too fibrous and tough to eat, but are useful for making soup stock. You can buy the mushrooms fresh or dried; the latter have a stronger flavor.

To reconstitute them, put them in very hot water for about 30 minutes, or until softened, drain (you can save the soaking water for flavoring a soup base), blot dry with paper towels, remove and discard the stems, and then cut as directed in individual recipes for fresh mushrooms.

Shiitakes are usually simmered in soups or cooked in stir-fries and are not normally eaten raw. The fresh mushrooms are a little pricey, and more and more regular markets are carrying them nowadays. If you have not already tried them, you should. Their earthy taste is unusual and appealing. Look for mushrooms that are not too damp and are free of soft spots. You can substitute cremini mushrooms, which will approximate the look and texture but will fall short in the flavor department. The price of dried shiitakes varies depending on their size and thickness. If they are $1/3$ to $1/2$ inch thick, they are juicer and more toothsome when they are reconstituted. Circumference is not as important as thickness, but you will spend a lot more time slicing small ones. Dried shiitakes keep well and are available online.

SOBA NOODLES
See Noodles.

SOY SAUCE
The most often used of all Japanese flavorings, soy sauce evokes much national pride. Naturally brewed from fermented soybeans, the sauce has a rich, yeasty, salty, deep flavor. Be aware that there are pretenders to soy sauce out there that are not soy sauce at all, but rather chemical flavorings. Kikkoman is a leading brand internationally and is widely available. I keep a large bottle of regular soy sauce in the refrigerator at all times. Other types are sold, such as a lighter-colored soy sauce that some cooks use because it appears more attractive in certain

dishes, as well as low-sodium and dark soy sauces. I used only regular soy sauce for the recipes in this book.

SUKIYAKI SAUCE
See Sauces.

TERIYAKI SAUCE
See Sauces.

TOFU
A lot of Westerners get turned off whenever anyone starts talking about tofu. They don't know how to cook it, they find the texture off-putting, they point out that it doesn't have much taste, and they resent its reputation of being "good for you." Taken together, these observations make tofu something they don't want to put on their "to try" list. If you are among the naysayers, you need to give tofu a chance. Make my recipes and you'll see that tofu is easy to use, that you can usually pick the

texture you like, and that it takes on the taste of the simmering liquid or sauce in which it is cooked (which, of course, is delicious!). And there is never anything wrong with eating healthful foods.

In Japan, fresh tofu is sold, immersed in water, at local tofu shops, and it has a clean, fresh taste and soft, almost creamy texture. The tofu available in the United States is reasonably good and inexpensive, and, yes, it is good for you. It comes in three basic types, firm, medium, and soft or silken, with the latter sometimes labeled *kinugoshi*. Markets sell tofu in shelf-stable boxes that need to be drained and then refrigerated after opening, or in plastic tubs that are refrigerated at the market. The tofu is usually, though not always, in a single large block, and the packages typically weigh 14 or 16 ounces. Always check the sell-by date on tofu packages. Tofu does not keep well once it is opened, so store it immersed in cold water in a clean, covered container in the refrigerator for no more than a couple of days, and change the water daily. It also takes on the flavor of whatever is around it, which is why you want to store it well covered and not near anything stinky.

TOMATO KETCHUP
See Sauces.

TONKATSU SAUCE
See Sauces.

TSUYU
See Sauces.

TURNIP
Small, white, mild-tasting Japanese turnips, or *kabu*, are used for pickling and for adding to soups and stews. Since Western turnips are usually larger than the golf ball–size specimens stocked in Japanese markets, buy the smallest, blemish-free turnips available and store them in a cool, dark place if you can. They become soggy if stored in the refrigerator for very long. If they do get soggy, peel them and soak them in a few changes of ice water or very cold water, before cutting as directed and using in recipes.

UDON NOODLES
See Noodles.

WASABI
This pungent green horseradish—no botanical relation to Western horseradish—is available as a paste in tubes or as a powder in small cans. If you buy a tube, once you open it, it must be refrigerated. To mix the powder, follow the package directions, which usually calls for stirring together a small

Shopping List

Stock your kitchen with the following items and you will be ready to make most of the recipes in this book.

Must Haves

Chili bean paste
Dashi
Mirin
Miso
Panko
Rice
Rice vinegar
Sake
Sesame oil
Soy sauce
Tonkatsu sauce
Worcestershire sauce

Frequently Used Ingredients

Cornstarch
Cucumber
    (Japanese or English)
Eggs
Eggplants
    (Japanese or Chinese)
Ginger
Garlic
Green onions
Ground beef, chicken,
    and pork
Kabocha pumpkin
Onions (yellow)
Tomato ketchup
Tofu

amount of the powder with a small amount of tepid water. Let it sit for a couple of minutes to allow the flavor to "bloom." Be careful when you eat wasabi. A little dab packs a powerful punch. It is a traditional condiment for sushi and is used in dipping sauces for noodles.

WORCESTERSHIRE SAUCE
See Sauces.

YAKISOBA SAUCE
See Sauces.

YELLOWTAIL
A type of snapper, known as *hamachi* when it is young and *buri* when it is more mature, yellowtail is an oily white fish but without a strong fishy taste. Used often in Japanese cooking, it is perfect for basting with teriyaki sauce and is frequently seen on sushi and sashimi menus.

Equipment

CHOPSTICKS
Found in Japanese restaurants everywhere, chopsticks, or *ohashi*, seem to make your Japanese food taste better and more authentic. They come in many materials—bamboo and other wood, plastic, metal—and styles and in a range of prices, with prized *hinoki*-wood chopsticks at the top of the pile. But chopsticks in any style will accomplish their main task of  ferrying your delicious cooking from bowl to mouth. *Waribashi* (disposable wooden chopsticks) are

inexpensive and can be bought by the pack. Or, you can look for *ohashi* that match your dishware and décor in many kitchen stores. Long cooking chopsticks, once you get the hang of working with them, are the best tools for turning hot foods, especially when frying.

At a place setting, *ohashi* should be laid horizontally below the main plate, with tips facing left for a right-handed person and right for a left-handed person. The tips are often placed on a chopstick rest— a small, decorated stand made of ceramic or other material—so that they don't touch the table.

Keep in mind the following rules of etiquette, too: Never leave your chopsticks stuck straight up in a bowl of rice, and don't use them to pass food to others, chopsticks to chopsticks. Both recall funeral customs. Also, never point with your chopsticks or spear your food with them. It's just not nice.

DROP-LID
Known as an *otoshi-buta*, this wooden lid, which has a small wooden handle on top, fits just inside of a pot rim. It floats directly on top of the simmering foods, keeping them from moving around, helping to spread the flavors of the liquid evenly, and preventing the liquid from cooking away. *Nimono* (simmered) dishes such as *Otoosan no Kabocha Nimono* (page 55) and *Iridori* (page 109) employ this specialized lid. I haven't bought one—no good reason, just haven't gotten around to it—so I make my own by shaping a disk of aluminum foil.

My substitution works passably well, except that you have to remember to use a potholder when fishing it out at the end of cooking, as it gets very hot. Also, it is also not as effective in making sure foods cook through evenly, which is another benefit of the *otoshi-buta*. An Asian kitchen supplies store or Web site will have drop-lids in different sizes to fit your pots.

GRATER
An inexpensive grater, or *oroshi*, is used for preparing ginger, daikon, and *yamaimo* (sticky mountain potato). The graters come with different-sized rasps, depending on what you are grating. Many of my recipes call for grated ginger, so I find the fine-rasp ginger grater particularly useful. It comes in ceramic, metal, or plastic. The ceramic ones are especially nice because they have a moat around the edge that captures all the tiny grated pieces and the valuable juice.

MANDOLINE
This kitchen device is great for slicing onions, potatoes, cucumbers, and cabbage very thinly with little effort. There are expensive mandolines on the market, but you can find inexpensive everyday slicers in well-stocked kitchenware stores. I like the ceramic blade slicer made  by Kyocera. I find I use it often, especially when using a knife would be too tedious and the job is too small for my food processor. As with any slicer, be very careful to keep your fingers clear of the blade when it is in use.

NABE
This earthenware cooking pot is traditionally used to make tabletop stews, such as Sukiyaki (page 134) and *Chankonabe* (page 107). If you have one, you can cook these dishes on your stove top and serve them at the table directly from the attractive clay pot (placed on a trivet, of course, to protect your tabletop).

RICE COOKER
This is your most essential piece of kitchen equipment. The rice cooker will enable you to cook rice quickly and easily. Many of these "smart" machines can adjust to the type of rice being cooked (white, brown, recent harvest, older), the cooking method (steam, boil, make into gruel), and the time that you want to have the rice ready. In other words, you can set the cooker to start while you're still at work and the rice will be done when you get home. Some rice cookers also have settings that will keep rice warm for use later in the day or even the next morning. If you are planning to cook Japanese or other Asian dishes with any frequency, purchase an electric rice cooker. Many kinds are readily available that are not too expensive, and even the most basic cooker will usually turn out better rice, faster and more reliably, than the stove-top method.

SURIBACHI
Nothing works better for grinding sesame seeds than a *suribachi*, a

ceramic grinding bowl lined with ridges, and a wooden pestle (*surikogi*)— the Japanese version of the mortar and pestle. The bowl, which is glazed on the outside and unglazed on the inside, comes in various sizes. A *suribachi* that measures about the diameter of a dinner plate is the most practical for the home cook. But a coffee grinder that you use only for seeds and spices or a mini food processor will also accomplish the task. The *suribachi* is useful for preparing foods from other cuisines as well, such as pesto, and for combining ingredients to make salad dressings, crushing garlic, and more.

WOK

You can find woks for sale in most kitchenware shops, and you don't need to spend a lot of money to get a quality product. They come in a variety of materials, including carbon steel and anodized aluminum, and in both regular and nonstick finishes. Their rounded bottoms and high sloped sides make it easy to toss foods rapidly for stir-frying, though they are equally well suited to deep-frying and steaming. A 12-inch wok is a practical size for most kitchens.

Tofu and Eggs

Tofu is a staple of the Japanese diet and has gained popularity elsewhere, too, first as a high-protein health food, and then because cooks have discovered how versatile—and tasty—it can be. Until I went to live in Japan, I didn't have a good idea of how to integrate tofu into my cooking. Once there, I saw how easy tofu is to use and I discovered the wide variety of dishes that can be made with it.

Tofu is available in the United States in three basic forms—soft, medium, and firm— and many regular markets stock at least two of them and sometimes all three. This trio of terms describes the consistency of the tofu. Soft, also called silken, is very soft, almost puddinglike, yet holds its shape, and is used for cold dishes like Hiyayakko (page 41) and in miso and other soups. The two firmer varieties hold their shape more easily, making them well suited to stir-fries and simmered dishes.

I have some friends who like the soft variety, and some who will eat nothing but firm tofu. The Kanekos are predisposed to

the silken variety. I have specified the tofu that I use or that is most commonly used in each recipe in this chapter, but for the most part, the texture that you like best is going to work fine for all of the recipes. Just don't use flavored, pressed, or smoked tofu. One of the great properties of tofu is its ability to take on the taste of what it is cooked with, so a flavored product would defeat that useful quality in these recipes.

Eggs are as versatile as tofu in Japanese cooking, turning up at every meal, rather than just at breakfast time. Variations on the traditional omelet are practically a whole cuisine in themselves, plus a number of other home-style dishes call for these inexpensive sources of high-quality protein for making batters, binding croquettes, coating foods for frying, and other uses.

Eggs in Japan are a little different than those I buy in the States. The first time I cracked open a Japanese egg I thought there was something wrong with it. Japanese eggs have dark yellow, nearly orange yolks with

a rich and rounded flavor. They're eaten all kinds of ways, from hard boiled to raw, and although I can't recommend that you eat raw eggs because of the risk of salmonella bacteria, Japanese cooks regularly top bowls of hot rice or soup with raw eggs or use them as a dipping sauce for meat dishes, such as sukiyaki (page 134). When the eggs are scrambled, they are usually cooked so that they form large, soft, delicate "curds," ensuring that their rich taste and pleasing texture become elements of the dish. And in so-called modern Japanese food, you'll find eggs sunny-side up on hamburgers or steaks or hard boiled and encased in egg-shaped mini chicken meat loaves.

left: *Agedashi Dofu*, page 26

Agedashi Dofu

Fried Soft Tofu in Gingery Sweet Soy Sauce

This recipe requires some physical dexterity but is otherwise quite simple. Soft tofu is very delicate and has to be handled carefully to keep from crushing it or breaking it into small pieces. However, once it has been weighted so that some of its water drains away, it is easier to work with. Also, the creamy interior and crispy coating of the fried tofu paired with the salty-sweet-gingery sauce tastes so wonderful that making this slightly tricky recipe is worth the trouble.

The sauce is a mildly sweet combination of dashi, mirin, and soy sauce called tsuyu. Bottled tsuyu is readily available; dilute it as directed for a noodle dipping sauce. Buy two packages of tofu in case one goes wrong, and know that even if the tofu breaks into small pieces, the pieces can still be fried if they measure at least an inch or more. If they cannot be fried, all is not lost: Simply put the cold tofu in a bowl and top with the sauce for Hiyayakko (page 41). Firmer tofu can be used (you still need to drain off the excess water, as you do for the soft tofu), but the texture will be less delicate.

1 package (14 ounces) soft tofu
Cornstarch for dusting
Canola or other neutral oil for deep-frying
2 green onions, including tender green tops,
    thinly sliced

2 teaspoons peeled and grated fresh ginger
¼ cup warmed tsuyu (page 19)

Carefully remove the block of tofu from its package. Cut it in half horizontally and then in half again crosswise. Place the tofu quarters in a single layer on several layers of paper towel on a large plate or cutting board. Top each quarter with several more layers of paper towel, and then top with a plate. Finally, put a weight, such as a can of tomatoes or something similar, on top of each stack. Let drain for about 30 minutes, changing the paper towels (very carefully) once after 15 minutes.

Remove the weight and the paper towels from each stack and pat the tofu dry. Place the pieces on a cutting board and cut them into 2-inch squares. Put some cornstarch in a small, shallow bowl and place it near the stove. Put the tofu next to the cornstarch.

Pour the oil to a depth of 3 inches into a deep, wide saucepan and heat to 350°F on a deep-frying thermometer or until bubbles immediately form around a wooden chopstick held upright in the pan. When the oil is ready, very gently dust 1 piece of tofu on all sides with the cornstarch and carefully place it in the hot oil. You can use your hand if you're brave, or a flat spoon if you're not. Repeat with additional squares, but do not crowd the pan, and do not dust the tofu until you are ready to fry it. Fry the tofu squares until the coating is crispy and firm (it will be lightly golden but not brown), 2 to 3 minutes. Using a slotted spatula, carefully remove the squares to paper towels to drain. Repeat until all the tofu is fried. (I usually serve each batch as it is ready—true home style—but the tofu will stay warm for a few minutes, and the warm sauce will heat up the tofu when you serve it.)

Place an equal number of tofu squares in each individual bowl and top with the green onions and ginger. Divide the warm tsuyu evenly between the bowls, pouring it into them just before serving so that the tofu doesn't get soggy. Serve right away.

Serves 2 generously as light main course, or 4 as an appetizer

Photo on page 24

Tea

One of the traditions I brought home with me from Japan was drinking tea. In nearly every Japanese home, you'll find a large thermos that dispenses hot water—ready to make tea at any time. In my mother-in-law's house, a strict tea schedule is in force: you get *ryokucha* (green tea) at breakfast, tea with the morning snack and more tea with the afternoon refreshment (both usually green tea), *genmai cha* (brown rice tea) or *hojicha* (roasted green tea) throughout the day, and *bancha* (tea with less caffeine) in the evening. My mother-in-law gave *mugicha* (caffeine-free cold barley tea) to all her grandchildren as early as their first year, and they got used to drinking it instead of fruit juice.

Traditionally, tea in Japan is never sweetened, and some varieties have a bitter, strong flavor that can take some getting used to. The Japanese (and now, the rest of the world) have long believed in drinking traditional teas for good health. However, sweetened "milk teas" are gaining popularity with young housewives and others, and nowadays you can buy them along with Chinese oolong or Japanese green tea or black *kohi* (coffee) in vending machines everywhere in Japan—both cold and hot!

While I can find green tea in markets here, I haven't quite returned to my mother-in-law's tea service schedule. I have noticed that a Japanese tea company, Ito-En, has started distributing some of my favorite teas (golden oolong and *hojicha*), already brewed in bottles, in some local markets, and whenever I see them, I buy them. Interestingly enough, while Shohei cannot do without his miso soup, he doesn't seem to miss drinking tea.

Mapo Dofu

Chinese-Style Spicy Tofu with Pork

Guys in particular like this hearty dish of tofu and pork in a spicy sauce, and it is great served with rice. The Japanese make a joke that husbands don't cook at all. Actually, they are known for being able to prepare a standard repertoire of "husband" recipes: curry rice (page 126), fried rice (page 145), and ramen noodle soup (page 155). I guess that I am luckier than most wives because Shohei likes to cook what he wants to eat. Fortunately for me, he has a wide-ranging appetite, and a first-rate **mapo dofu** is among his specialties.

Mapo dofu is also found in Chinese restaurants in Japan, and many lunch counters serve a **mapo dofu** rice plate, which is how you should serve it at home—with a big bowl of rice. Sometimes Shohei likes to change it up a bit and makes **Mapo Nasu** (page 56), with deep-fried eggplant instead of the tofu. It's also great. You'll note that a couple of Chinese bottled sauces are used in this recipe. Most well-stocked supermarkets carry these, or they can also easily be ordered online. If you can't find the chili bean paste, you can use chili garlic paste or chili garlic sauce, though the soybeans in the chili bean paste add a wonderful deep, rich flavor to this dish. You can use medium or firm tofu, if you like, but the texture will be crumbly, closer to that of the pork, denying you the contrast between the soft tofu and the rough-textured pork.

6 green onions
3 cloves garlic, minced
1-inch piece fresh ginger, peeled and minced

Sauce
2 teaspoons chili bean paste
1/2 cup reduced-fat, low-sodium canned chicken broth
1 teaspoon oyster sauce
1 tablespoon soy sauce
1 tablespoon sake

1 teaspoon sugar
2 teaspoons cornstarch dissolved in 2 teaspoons water
About 1 teaspoon sesame oil

2 tablespoons canola or other neutral oil
1/2 pound ground pork
2 packages (14 ounces each) soft tofu, drained
3 cups hot cooked rice (see **Gohan**, page 140)

Mince the white parts and tender green tops of 4 green onions, and then mince the white part only of the remaining 2 green onions. Cut the tender green tops of these last 2 onions in half lengthwise, and then cut crosswise into 1-inch lengths. Place the minced green onion, garlic, and ginger in 3 small separate bowls. Set the green onion tops aside separately.

Ready the sauce ingredients. Measure the chili bean paste into a small bowl. In another small bowl, stir together the chicken broth, oyster sauce, soy sauce, sake, and sugar. Set the bowls near the stove. Have the cornstarch-water mixture and the bottle of sesame oil near the stove as well.

continued

Place a wok or large frying pan over high heat. When it is hot, add the canola oil and swirl the pan to coat the bottom and sides with the oil. When the oil is very hot, add the garlic and cook, stirring constantly with a spatula so it doesn't burn, until fragrant. Then add the ginger and minced green onions, stir well, and reduce the heat to medium. Add the ground pork and continue to stir constantly, breaking up the pork and integrating it with the other ingredients. When the pork is just cooked, after about 2 minutes, add the chili bean paste and pour in the stock mixture. Using the spatula, combine all the ingredients well with the sauce.

Place the tofu in the pan and, using the edge of a ladle or a spoon, cut it into large chunks. Cook over medium heat until the tofu is heated through, about 2 minutes. Stir the water-cornstarch mixture to recombine, pour it slowly into the pan, and then stir gently until the liquid in the pan thickens and becomes glossy, about 1 minute. Drizzle in a little sesame oil and garnish with the reserved green onion tops.

Spoon the tofu-and-pork mixture into a serving bowl or onto a platter, family style, and serve each diner a bowl of rice. Or, spoon the mixture over individual bowls of rice and serve.

Serves 4

Izakaya

An *izakaya* is the Japanese equivalent of the bar or pub, a place where people go for drinking and camaraderie. These casual spots also serve food to accompany the beer, sake, or *shochu* (a vodka-like spirit). Usually the food is small dishes, known collectively as *ippin ryori*, a sort of Japanese "tapas," such as *hiyayakko* (page 41), *kara-age* (page 110), potato salad (page 72), and simple slices of cooked fish or meat, or sashimi (but never sushi).

Kanitama

Chinese-Style Crab Omelet with Soy Sauce Gravy

The savory gravy is what distinguishes this large, fluffy crab omelet. This Chinese-inspired (chuka ryori) omelet is an example of Japanese home-style cooking borrowing liberally from another cuisine and refashioning the recipe to Japanese taste. Many of these adaptations go together quickly and call for only simple techniques and a handful of ingredients, characteristics that particularly appeal to young Japanese housewives.

You can cook kanitama in a large frying pan, but a wok is better because it gives you more room to move the eggs around. You can serve it as is, or over rice, to make kanitama donburi.

4 large eggs
Pinch of salt
½ cup crabmeat (fresh or canned), picked over for shell fragments and cartilage
2 tablespoons chopped bamboo shoots
2 green onions, including tender green tops, minced
2 fresh shiitake mushrooms, stems discarded and caps thinly sliced
1 tablespoon frozen peas

Sauce
½ cup reduced-fat, low-sodium canned chicken broth
1½ teaspoons soy sauce
1½ teaspoons sugar
¼ teaspoon sake
Pinch of salt
1½ teaspoons cornstarch dissolved in 1½ teaspoons water

2 tablespoons canola or other neutral oil
½ teaspoon sesame oil

Break the eggs into a large bowl and beat with a fork or chopsticks until well blended. Stir in the salt and then add the crabmeat, bamboo shoots, green onions, mushrooms, and peas and mix thoroughly. Set aside.

To make the sauce, in a small saucepan, combine the chicken broth, soy sauce, sugar, sake, and salt and bring to a rolling simmer over medium heat. Stir the water-cornstarch mixture to recombine, pour slowly into the pan, and cook, stirring, until thickened, 1 to 2 minutes. Set the sauce aside on another burner turned to the lowest heat setting.

Place a wok or large frying pan over high heat. When it is hot, add the canola oil and swirl the pan to coat the bottom and sides with the oil. When the oil is very hot, add the egg mixture. When it hits the pan, it will make a sizzling sound. Add the sesame oil and, using a wooden spatula, stir the egg mixture constantly, lifting and pushing the edges so that the uncooked portion flows underneath. When the omelet is completely cooked but still soft, pile it in the center of the wok and let the bottom cook until the mass is solidified and the bottom is lightly browned, another 1 to 2 minutes. The top should still be quite soft. Slide the omelet into a large, shallow bowl and immediately ladle the warm sauce over the top. Eat with a spoon.

Serves 2

Tofu no Soboro Ankake

Tofu with Gingery Chicken Sauce

Here is a protein-rich variation on Nasu no Soboro Ankake (page 61), with tofu substituted for the eggplant. Because the tofu is simply simmered briefly in a seasoned broth and not fried, this dish is lighter and also quicker to prepare. The soft tofu is delicate and breaks easily, so the cube size is quite large. If you like, you can instead use medium or firm tofu.

Sauce
3/4 pound ground chicken
1 cup plus 2 tablespoons water
2 tablespoons plus 3/4 teaspoon soy sauce
1 teaspoon ginger juice (page 16)
1 teaspoon mirin
1 tablespoon plus 3/4 teaspoon sugar
1 tablespoon cornstarch dissolved in
    5 teaspoons water

2 cups reduced-fat, low-sodium canned
    chicken broth
1 teaspoon soy sauce
1 teaspoon salt
2 teaspoons sugar
1 package (16 ounces) soft tofu, drained and
    cut into 4 equal cubes

To make the sauce, in a saucepan, combine the chicken, water, 2 tablespoons plus 3/4 teaspoon soy sauce, ginger juice, mirin, and 1 tablespoon plus 3/4 teaspoon sugar and place over medium heat. Cook, stirring often and breaking up the chicken with a wooden spoon, until the chicken is no longer pink, about 5 minutes. Stir the water-cornstarch mixture to recombine and then pour slowly into the pan and stir until the sauce thickens, about 1 minute. Remove from the heat and set aside.

In a saucepan large enough to accommodate the tofu in a single layer, combine the chicken broth, 1 teaspoon soy sauce, salt, and 2 teaspoons sugar. Bring to a boil over high heat and gently add the tofu. Reduce the heat to medium and cook for 5 minutes to season the tofu and heat through. While the tofu is cooking, gently reheat the sauce.

Using a slotted spoon, carefully transfer the tofu cubes to individual bowls, putting 1 cube in each bowl. Top each serving with an equal amount of the sauce and serve hot.

Serves 4

Tamago Toji Jiru

Stirred Egg Soup

Tamago toji jiru is the first—and easiest—recipe that okaasan (honored mother—or, in my case, mother-in-law) shared with me, after we had eaten it as part of breakfast one morning. Even okaasan uses dashi-no-moto, or instant dashi, rather than cooking up a batch of dashi from scratch. You can serve this soup at any meal of the day. I have included the proportions for a single serving, but you can easily multiply them to accommodate any number of eaters.

1 medium egg
1 cup dashi or reduced-fat, low-sodium
    canned chicken broth
½ teaspoon sake
Pinch of salt

1 green onion, white part and tender green
    tops, thinly sliced lengthwise and then
    cut crosswise into thirds
⅛ teaspoon sesame oil (optional)

Break the egg into a small bowl and beat lightly just until blended; set aside. In a small saucepan, bring the dashi to a rolling simmer over medium heat. Add the sake and salt. Then, using chopsticks or a fork, stir the egg into the broth and swirl the pan for about 30 seconds. The egg will set in long threads. Add the green onion and remove from the heat.

Drizzle in the sesame oil for aroma, if you like. Pour into a bowl and serve immediately.

Serves 1

Okonomiyaki

"As You Like It" Pancake

Okonomiyaki, literally "grilled as you like it," originated as home-style food in Osaka. It calls for mixing vegetables, meat, fish, or shellfish into a batter, cooking the batter, and then topping the finished pancake with a Worcestershire-style sauce and mayonnaise. The ingredients and combinations can be customized to individual tastes and almost anything goes. Thinly sliced fatty pork, bacon, and shrimp are popular additions, as are squid, chicken, beef, vegetables, cheese, scallops, and so on. Okonomiyaki is often served with yakisoba (page 152), and Hiroshima-style okonomiyaki marries the two into a sort of noodle-filled pancake.

Okonomiyaki is easy to prepare at home and is a crowd-pleaser, especially for kids. A griddle is great for cooking this dish, but a frying pan can be used, too. The disadvantage to the latter is that while a griddle allows you to prepare at least two pancakes at once, a frying pan limits you to one pancake at a time. Let each diner drizzle on as much sauce and mayonnaise as he or she wants. And be sure to eat the pancakes while they are hot.

10 slices thick-cut bacon
1 cup all-purpose flour
½ teaspoon baking powder
Pinch of salt
1 cup minus 1 tablespoon water
2 large eggs
½ medium green head cabbage, shredded or coarsely chopped
1 green onion, including tender green tops, thinly sliced

5 shrimp, boiled for about 3 minutes until cooked throughout, drained, peeled, and cut into small pieces
4 tablespoons canola or other neutral oil

For Serving
1 cup **okonomiyaki** or **tonkatsu** sauce (page 19)
¼ cup mayonnaise
Aonori or shredded **yakinori** (page 18) and **katsuobushi** (see note)

Preheat the oven to 275°F and have ready a rimmed baking sheet (this is for keeping the cooked pancakes warm until they are all cooked).

Lay the bacon slices between 2 or so layers of paper towel and microwave on high for 3 minutes. The bacon will not be completely cooked, but some of the fat will have been rendered and absorbed by the towels. Alternatively, cook the bacon in a frying pan over medium-high heat, turning as needed, for 4 to 5 minutes to achieve the same result. Cut each bacon slice into 4 equal pieces and set aside.

In a large bowl, using a fork or chopsticks, stir together the flour, baking powder, salt, and water. Beat in the eggs until well mixed. Stir in the cabbage, green onion, and shrimp.

Place a 10-inch nonstick frying pan over medium-high heat. When it is hot, add 1 tablespoon of the oil and swirl to coat the bottom of the pan. When the oil is hot, arrange 5 pieces of

continued

the bacon in a circle roughly 6 inches in diameter in the center of the pan. Then, using a ladle, immediately spread one-fourth of the batter over the circle of bacon to create a pancake about 6 inches in diameter and 1 inch thick. Press 5 more pieces of bacon into the top of the pancake. Cook, without disturbing, until just browned on the bottom, about 5 minutes. At this point, the pancake should easily slide in the pan. Do not be tempted to flip it before it is set! Using a spatula, flip the pancake and cook on the second side until browned, 4 to 5 minutes longer. Transfer the pancake to the baking sheet and place in the oven to keep warm. Repeat with the remaining bacon pieces, batter, and oil to make 3 more pancakes, keeping each one warm in the oven as it comes out of the pan.

When all the pancakes are cooked, transfer 2 of the pancakes to individual plates and leave the others in the oven. (Or, you can cook 2 pancakes, eat them, and then cook the remaining 2 pancakes.) Have the sauce, mayonnaise, nori, and katsuobushi in small separate bowls on the table. Each diner drizzles as much sauce and mayonnaise onto the pancake as he or she wants and then tops it with nori and finally with the katsuobushi. If the okonomiyaki is properly hot, the katsuobushi will seem to dance. When the first pancakes have been eaten, serve the remaining 2 pancakes.

Serves 2

Note: Katsuobushi, the same dried bonito flakes used for making dashi from scratch, are also a popular topping for Hiyayakko (page 41), Yakisoba (page 152), or yudofu (simmered tofu). They are most commonly sold in small individual packets (or several individual packets in a box), which should be stored in a cool, dry cupboard. The flavor and aroma of the flakes dissipate fairly quickly once a packet is opened.

Takoyaki

Takoyaki, a specialty of Osaka and of Kyoto, is a wonderful variation on Okonomiyaki. The same basic batter (minus the cabbage and other additions) is cooked in a special pan with round molds about two inches in diameter. The batter is poured into each hole and then a small piece of boiled octopus and perhaps a little green onion and some slivered, bright pink beni shoga (pickled ginger) are poked into the center. When the bottoms have solidified, each ball is carefully lifted with a toothpick and flipped to the other side to cook, resulting in a perfect sphere. When the balls are done, the outside is pancake-like and crisp, while the inside is soft and almost molten—a delicious contrast.

Takoyaki are served in little trays of six pieces, and they are garnished with the same sauces, nori, and katsuobushi as okonomiyaki. It is tempting to eat them immediately, but you must be careful, as the insides are very hot! They are a common sight at street festivals and at yatai (street-food stalls). My favorite time to eat them is at New Year, after my husband, his extended family, our children, and I have all made the long, cold trek to the local shrine for our New Year's blessing. On the walk back to the car, we always pass a takoyaki stand, and those piping-hot snacks are the perfect food at the perfect time.

Gomoku Iridofu

Tofu with "Five Things"

This is a popular one-dish Japanese meal that is also good for you. I have often seen it in the prepared-food counters at department stores and just as often on my mother-in-law's table. The custom of "five things" carries over to other dishes, too, such as gomoku gohan (rice with five things) and gomoku soba (soba noodles with five things). Inexplicably, the use of the term "five things" doesn't always mean that a dish includes exactly that number of different foods. Often you will discover that there are only four or as many as seven different items. But the number five does play an important role in Japanese cuisine. A classic balanced meal traditionally includes five flavors, five types of food preparation, and five colors. Elizabeth Andoh's beautiful book Washoku has more on this tradition.

Gobo or burdock, a fibrous root vegetable, is one of the typical ingredients in this dish, but because it is difficult to find, I've substituted bamboo shoots, which are also crunchy. It is important to put the snow peas in ice water after blanching them, so that they remain crisp and bright green.

1 package (16 ounces) medium or firm tofu

3 fresh shiitake mushrooms, stems discarded and caps thinly sliced

1 boneless, skinless chicken thigh, visible fat removed and cut into 1/2-inch pieces

1 small carrot, peeled and chopped

2 tablespoons chopped bamboo shoots

1 tablespoon soy sauce

1 1/2 teaspoons sugar

Pinch of salt

1 large egg, lightly beaten

2 green onions, including tender green tops, chopped

8 to 10 snow peas, trimmed, blanched in boiling water for 1 minute, drained, immersed in ice water, drained again, and slivered lengthwise

Open the tofu package and transfer both the tofu and the liquid to a large saucepan. Place over medium heat and use a wooden spoon or spatula to break up the tofu into large chunks. As soon as it is broken up, add the mushrooms, chicken, carrot, and bamboo shoots and cook, stirring, until the chicken just loses its pink color, 4 to 5 minutes. Add the soy sauce, sugar, and salt, stir to mix, and then add the egg. Continue to stir until the egg has set in small pieces, about 3 minutes. By this time the tofu will have broken up into smaller pieces, the vegetables should be tender, and the chicken should be cooked through. Add the green onions and mix one more time.

Serve piping hot family style or in individual bowls. Garnish with the snow peas.

Serves 4

Omu Raisu

Omelet Stuffed with Tomatoey Chicken Rice

Every basic Japanese cookbook and cooking show includes instructions for making this simple stuffed omelet, which epitomizes *yoshoku* cuisine. Very quick to make and exceptionally tasty, **omu raisu** is served by moms, school cafeterias, and high- and low-end restaurants. Some places in Tokyo serve nothing but this dish and offer many different fillings or a choice of curry sauce (page 126) or hayashi beef sauce (page 124) spooned over the top.

This filling is a great way to use up leftover cooked rice. The omelet should still be soft in the middle when the filling is added, and then it should be carefully flipped over the filling, so that each diner is presented with a football-shaped yellow omelet topped with a squiggle of ketchup and a sprig of parsley. The texture of the soft egg combined with the tomatoey rice is sublime. Tiny steamed and buttered potatoes and steamed broccoli are good accompaniments.

Filling
1 tablespoon unsalted butter
1 boneless, skinless chicken thigh, cut into
    ½-inch pieces
¼ cup chopped fresh white mushrooms
½ yellow onion, minced
1½ cups cooked rice (see **Gohan**, page 140),
    cold or at room temperature
¼ cup tomato ketchup, plus more for garnish
¼ cup low-fat, reduced-sodium canned
    chicken broth

½ teaspoon salt
Ground pepper

Omelets
6 large eggs
2 tablespoons whole or low-fat milk
½ teaspoon salt
1 tablespoon unsalted butter

2 fresh parsley sprigs (optional)

To make the filling, in a large frying pan, melt ½ tablespoon of the butter over medium heat. When the butter is hot, add the chicken and cook, stirring often, until the chicken is half cooked, about 2 minutes. Add the mushrooms and cook, stirring often, until the chicken is cooked through and the mushrooms are tender, 2 to 3 minutes longer. Transfer to a bowl and set aside.

Return the pan to medium heat and add the remaining ½ tablespoon butter. When it melts, add the onion and cook, stirring often, until translucent, about 5 minutes. Add the rice and, using a wooden spatula, press against it to separate the grains. Cook for about 1 minute, stirring to prevent sticking, and then add the ¼ cup tomato ketchup, chicken broth, and chicken mixture and cook until all the liquid is absorbed, about 3 minutes longer. Add the ½ teaspoon salt and pepper to taste, remove from the heat, and cover to keep warm.

To make the first omelet, in a bowl, combine 3 of the eggs, 1 tablespoon of the milk, and ¼ teaspoon of the salt and beat with a fork or chopsticks until well blended.

continued

In a 10-inch omelet pan or nonstick frying pan, melt ½ tablespoon of the butter over medium heat. When it melts and the foam subsides, add the egg mixture and swirl the pan to spread it evenly. Using a fork, scramble quickly for about 30 seconds and then swirl the pan again so the eggs coat the entire bottom. Continue to cook, lifting the edges of the eggs occasionally to allow the uncooked portion to flow underneath. When the eggs are mostly set and just a little wet on top, after 3 to 4 minutes, add half of the filling, positioning it on one-half of the omelet, and then tip the pan so that the eggs fold over to encase the filling as the finished omelet slides onto a plate. You may need to use the spatula to help the final transport to the plate.

Cover the omelet with a paper towel and gently shape it into its characteristic football shape, removing some of the moisture in the process. Top with a squiggle of ketchup and with a parsley sprig, if desired. Repeat to make a second omelet with the remaining ingredients. Serve the omelets hot.

Serves 2

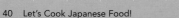

Hiyayakko

Cold Tofu with Ginger and Green Onions

I started making this simple combination of tofu topped with green onions and salty soy sauce on my very first stay in Japan, before I even met my husband. Soft tofu is widely available, and the preparation is so easy that I mastered it right away. The dish is perfect for serving on a warm day, and I have even seen the tofu served over ice for the ultimate cooling appetizer. Young children love the dish, too, since the tofu is so easy to swallow and the taste is so mild. Soft tofu was my daughters' favorite food from the moment they started eating solids.

Hiyayakko can be served as an appetizer, a side dish, or as one of a variety of small dishes called **ippin ryori** (lots of little things) that is typical **izakaya** food (page 30). At some **izakaya**, **momen** ("cotton," or firm) tofu is used, though I much prefer the texture of **kinugoshi** (soft or silken) tofu for this dish. Of course, the higher the quality of the tofu, the better the dish is, but supermarket-quality tofu will produce satisfactory results. I have given the amounts of each ingredient for a single serving, which you can easily adjust to the number of diners.

4-inch square soft tofu
1 teaspoon peeled and grated fresh ginger
1 tablespoon minced green onion,
    including tender green tops
¼ to ½ teaspoon soy sauce, preferably
    light soy sauce

Place the tofu in a shallow bowl. Arrange the ginger in a mound on the top of the tofu, and sprinkle with the green onion. Let the diner top with soy sauce according to his or her taste.

Serves 1

Tamagoyaki

Sweet Rolled Omelet

A mom classic, this simple rolled omelet with a bit of sweetness is a popular breakfast food, but it also appears regularly in lunch boxes and at sushi bars. Some say you can judge the skill of a sushi chef by the quality of his **tamagoyaki**. Mastering the rolling technique usually takes a few tries, but the failed attempts still taste good. And once you have it down pat, the slices of rolled omelet look impressive as appetizers or any way you choose to serve them. Though not traditional, I like to sprinkle chopped spinach, white cheese, or crumbled **yakinori** (page 18) on top of the omelet before I roll it up. When I cut the roll, the filling provides a pretty contrasting swirl at the center of each slice.

The Japanese have a specially designed rectangular omelet pan for this dish, which makes forming a neat roll easier than if you use a round pan. But many Japanese use a regular non-stick frying pan and I do too.

4 large eggs
3½ tablespoons dashi
1 tablespoon sugar

1½ teaspoons soy sauce
Pinch of salt
1 tablespoon canola or other neutral oil

In a bowl, combine the eggs, dashi, sugar, soy sauce, and salt and beat until well blended.

In a rectangular omelet pan or a 10-inch nonstick frying pan, heat ½ tablespoon of the canola oil over medium-high heat. Add one-third of the egg mixture and swirl the pan to spread the egg evenly. Let cook, lifting the edges of the eggs occasionally to allow the uncooked portion to flow underneath, until the bottom is firm but not browned, about 2 minutes. You do not want it to color. If the egg seems to be cooking and browning too quickly, reduce the heat to medium. Using chopsticks or a spatula, carefully lift one edge (a narrow edge if using a rectangular pan) of the omelet and, using your fingers to guide it gently, roll the egg away from you as tightly as you can without tearing it. Once the egg is in a roll at the far edge of the pan, add ¾ teaspoon of the remaining oil and half of the remaining egg. Gently lift the roll already created to allow a little of the liquid egg mixture to flow underneath. Cook the newly added egg in the same way as the first roll. When the bottom is firm but not browned, start with the already created roll (it becomes the core) and roll it away from you, wrapping the second egg sheet around it as you roll. The roll will again be at the far edge of the pan. Repeat the process one last time with the remaining ¾ teaspoon oil and the remaining egg mixture. You will now have a large roll.

Carefully remove the roll to a paper towel. Cover the top with another paper towel and gently press evenly on the roll to remove excess oil and moisture and to reinforce the shape. Let the omelet cool completely, then slice into rounds about 1½ inches thick. Serve at room temperature.

Serves 2

Miso Shiru

Miso Soup

When I moved to Japan, miso soup was not unfamiliar to me. At most Japanese restaurants in the States, a set meal invariably begins with a small bowl of the iconic soup. (In restaurants in Japan, miso soup is traditionally served at the end of the meal.) Sadly, in too many places, the miso shiru is the product of an inexpensive packet that holds the entire soup, minus the liquid, in desiccated form. The best "instant" miso soup brands have a dry packet of tofu, seaweed, or other ingredients, and then a packet of miso paste with broth flavoring. These are, to be honest, not bad. However, at my mother-in-law's I learned that making your own miso soup is not only easy, but also allows you to customize it to your own taste with the ingredients you have on hand. My favorite addition is small pieces of cooked kabocha pumpkin; my husband favors tiny, slippery nameko mushrooms. My mother-in-law usually takes the quick route and uses tofu, cooked potato, and onion.

A bowl of rice, a bowl of miso soup, and tsukemono (pickles) are a complete basic meal, as Japanese college students on a limited budget can attest. The key to maintaining the aroma and taste of the miso is not to overcook it and never to allow the soup to come to a boil. If you make the dashi from scratch, you need konbu, a type of kelp, and katsuobushi, or dried bonito flakes, which can be difficult to find if you don't have a Japanese market nearby. I use instant dashi with good results. I buy hondashi granules and keep the jar or packets in my refrigerator at all times. If you can't find the dashi when you need it, reduced-fat vegetable or even chicken broth, diluted with an equal amount of water (the soup base should not have a strong taste), can be substituted.

3 cups dashi

¼ cup miso, preferably white miso

½ block soft tofu, about 7 ounces, cut into
    ½-inch cubes

2 green onions, including tender green tops,
    minced

Pinch of dried **wakame**, reconstituted
    (optional; see note)

In a small saucepan, bring the dashi to a boil. Reduce the heat to medium so that the dashi is at a gentle simmer. To prevent the miso from forming salty lumps in your soup, put 1 tablespoon of the miso into a large spoon and, holding the spoon in one hand and a pair of chopsticks in the other, dip the edge of the spoon into the hot broth, scooping up a little of it onto the spoon. Holding the spoon above the broth, stir together the miso and dashi with the chopsticks to dissolve the miso, and then add it to the pan. Repeat with the remaining 3 tablespoons miso.

When all of the miso has been mixed in, add the tofu cubes and heat through, about 1 minute. Then add the green onions and the **wakame** (if using) and cook for 30 seconds longer. Remember, once the miso is in the pan, the soup must never boil.

Divide the soup among 4 bowls and serve piping hot.

Serves 4

Note: Wakame, a type of seaweed recognized for its healthful nutrients and used primarily in soups and salads, is almost always sold dried. To reconstitute it, soak it in warm water for 20 to 30 minutes and then add to the soup.

Vegetables

I'm always looking for ways to get more vegetables into my family's diet. In Japanese cuisine, vegetables are not just an afterthought at the side of the plate. Instead, they often occupy several of the little plates that are served with every meal. My father-in-law takes pride in the small garden in front of his house, and the daikon and other vegetables that he grows there and stores in the back shed appear nightly on the dinner table.

When I lived in Tokyo, I loved to shop at the local **yao-ya** (vegetable store), where the proprietor would give me suggestions on what to cook and how to cook it. One thing that I learned right away about vegetable shopping in Japan is that I was not to touch the produce on display. Rather, I was to point to my choice and let the clerk lift it out and hand it to me. It is no wonder that the displays of vegetables and fruits in Japan are so perfect.

Most of the recipes in this book call for vegetables, but the recipes in this chapter are favorites in which the vegetables are the focus of the dish. A little meat is often added to these dishes to enhance them, but the vegetables remain the stars. In general, Japanese like their vegetables cooked or pickled, rather than raw or in salads, and this chapter reflects that tradition. It also illustrates that average cooks use a lot of creativity to devise new and delicious ways to serve the bounty of vegetables available to them.

left: *Corn Shoyu-yaki*, page 48

Corn Shoyu-yaki

Grilled Corn on the Cob, Japanese Style

When corn is cooked over a fire, the kernels brown and caramelize, becoming absolutely delicious. I discovered this only when I brought home some corn, boiled in my usual way, and slathered it with butter. My husband took an uncooked ear, grilled it along with our hamburgers, and drizzled it with a little soy sauce, explaining to me that this was the Japanese way. And as with many of the discoveries I made in learning about his cuisine, his way was a keeper.

I have since come up with ways to prepare this very simple side dish when I don't have the outdoor grill fired up, including broiling it in the oven or in the toaster oven, or even cooking it in a frying pan with a little bit of oil. The big difference in texture and flavor—not mushy, almost crunchy, deliciously caramelized—comes from keeping the corn away from water and using little or no fat. At the table, the sweet corn taste is nicely balanced by the salty bite of the soy sauce. No butter is needed.

4 ears corn, shucked
Soy sauce

Prepare a hot fire in a charcoal grill, preheat a gas grill to high, or preheat a broiler.

If using a grill, place the corn directly over the fire and grill, turning as needed, until all the kernels are a mixture of dark brown and dark yellow, 5 to 7 minutes. If using a broiler, position the rack as close as possible to the heat source, arrange the corn on a broiler pan, and broil, turning as needed, for about 15 minutes. The kernels will color the same way.

Transfer the corn to a platter and serve immediately. Let each diner drizzle on soy sauce to taste. Be careful not to burn the roof of your mouth.

Serves 4 as a side dish

Photo on page 46

Horenso no Goma-ae

Spinach in Sesame Dressing

Lightly cooked spinach with a sweet, nutty dressing is one of the most popular vegetable dishes to make its way from Japan to the rest of the world. When I first arrived in Japan this was my go-to dish—at a restaurant, at home, in the supermarket take-out section—because I was trying to eat my vegetables (good girl!) and also because it looked fairly familiar.

The sesame dressing, known as goma-ae, can be found in Japanese restaurants everywhere outside of Japan, but it is often overly sweet and sometimes made with peanut butter instead of ground sesame seeds. Grinding the sesame seeds in a traditional suribachi (see page 22) is a great way to vent the stresses of the day and yields a wonderful fragrance as the seeds are crushed. You will want to eat this dressing on everything: I like it on green beans that are cooked tender crisp and still bright green, on cold shredded chicken, on steamed broccoli, or even on shelled edamame (page 15). Kids will eat any vegetable with this sauce on it.

1 large bunch spinach
Ice water as needed

Dressing
¼ cup sesame seeds, toasted (see page 20)
1½ tablespoons sugar
1½ tablespoons soy sauce
1½ teaspoons sake

Rinse the spinach leaves thoroughly in several changes of water and dry with paper towels. Then lay the leaves on paper towels, with root ends lined up (they will be trimmed later).

To make the dressing, using a suribachi, grind the sesame seeds into a rough powder. Add the sugar and grind again briefly to combine. Set aside.

Fill a large bowl with ice water and set aside. Bring a large pot of water to a boil and add the spinach, roots first, submerging the leaves in the water. Cook for 30 seconds, and then, using tongs or chopsticks, quickly transfer the spinach to the bowl of ice water, doing your best to keep the spinach roots aligned. This ice-water dip will stop the cooking and preserve the bright green color. Using your hands, squeeze the excess water from the spinach and then chop the leaves crosswise, cutting them into 4 or 5 short lengths and discarding the roots.

Transfer the sesame seed–sugar mixture to a large bowl. Add the soy sauce and sake and stir to mix well. Add the spinach and mix to combine the dressing thoroughly with the spinach. The spinach should be generously coated but not wet. Serve in individual bowls.

Serves 2 generously as a side dish

Potato Korokke

Potato Croquettes

Unbelievably crispy on the outside, and all fluffy, creamy deliciousness on the inside, korokke are beloved throughout Japan. Once the Japanese adapted the French croquette, they created endless variations on the theme, from this basic potato filling to pumpkin (page 52), corn (see variations, page 85 and facing page), crabmeat (page 84), tofu, and many more. In small towns and in cities near commuter train stations, korokke shops display a huge variety of fried items that the Japanese housewife can take home for a meal, adding her own side dishes, miso soup, and rice. Because deep-frying is easier when there is plenty of counter space to work on, it's not a common cooking method in most Japanese homes, where kitchens tend to be small. This basic recipe for korokke works well in a typical Western kitchen, allowing you to enjoy this popular Japanese food in the absence of the ubiquitous korokke shops of Japan. (For tips on deep-frying, see page 57.) Serve these croquettes with a generous pile of shredded green cabbage on the side, rice, and Miso Shiru (page 44).

4 russet potatoes, about 2 pounds total weight
1 tablespoon plus ¼ teaspoon salt
1 tablespoon canola or other neutral oil, plus oil for deep-frying
½ large yellow onion, minced
½ pound ground beef

⅛ teaspoon ground pepper, or more to taste
1 cup all-purpose flour
2 large eggs
2 to 3 cups **panko** (page 18)
Karashi (page 16) for serving
Tonkatsu sauce (page 19) for serving

In a large saucepan, combine the potatoes and 1 tablespoon salt with water to cover by 1 to 2 inches, place over high heat, and bring to a boil. Adjust the heat to maintain a gentle boil and cook the potatoes, uncovered, until a skewer or chopstick can easily pierce all the way through a potato and the potatoes are very soft, 45 minutes to 1 hour.

While the potatoes are cooking, in a frying pan, heat the 1 tablespoon oil over medium heat. When the oil is hot, add the onion and cook, stirring often, until translucent, 4 to 5 minutes. Add the ground beef and cook, breaking it up with a wooden spatula or spoon, until the meat is no longer pink, about 4 minutes longer. Add the 1/4 teaspoon salt and the pepper, mix well, and remove from the heat. Set aside.

When the potatoes are ready, using tongs, remove them from the water. Then, hold the potatoes in a clean, dry kitchen towel and rub gently to peel away the skins. Put the peeled potatoes in a large bowl and mash with a potato masher or the back of a fork until fairly smooth. Add the beef mixture and mix well. Let the mixture cool a bit before shaping and coating with the breading.

Spread the flour in a small, shallow bowl. Break the eggs into a second small, shallow bowl and beat with chopsticks or a fork until well blended. Spread about 2 cups **panko** in a third shallow bowl. Spread a little **panko** on a flat plate or tray.

Dampen your hands with water and form the potato mixture into 12 flat oblong shapes, about 3 inches long and 1 inch thick, packing them tightly. Gently dust each croquette with the flour, shaking off the excess; coat with the egg; and then coat with the panko, lightly pressing the panko in place with your fingertips. As each croquette is coated, set it aside on the panko-lined plate. As you work, add more panko to the bowl as needed. (At this point you can freeze the croquettes: arrange them on a platter or rimmed baking sheet, place in the freezer, and then transfer the frozen croquettes to a zippered plastic bag and return to the freezer for up to 3 months. You can deep-fry them directly from the freezer, but keep the oil temperature at 325° to 350°F and watch carefully to be sure the coating doesn't brown too quickly. I usually start the cooking at 350°F and then lower it if the coating is cooking too fast. The croquettes will still be very crispy, but the crumb coating will look flatter than the coating on fried freshly made croquettes.)

Pour the oil to a depth of 3 inches into a wok or deep, wide saucepan and heat to 350°F on a deep-frying thermometer or until a bit of panko dropped into the hot oil rises immediately to the top. Working in batches of 4 croquettes, drop the croquettes into the oil one at a time and fry until medium brown and crispy, about 8 minutes. Using tongs, remove the croquettes from the oil and drain on a wire rack or on paper towels.

Serve the croquettes hot. Provide each diner with a dab of karashi. Pass the tonkatsu sauce at the table for drizzling over or dipping the croquettes. Any leftovers can be eaten at room temperature for lunch the next day.

Makes 12 croquettes; serves 12 as an appetizer or 4 as a main course

Corn Korokke (Corn Croquettes) Variation: Substitute 1 cup corn kernels, either fresh or well-drained thawed, frozen, for the beef. Cook the onion as directed until translucent, and then add the corn, stir briefly to combine, and season as directed with the salt and pepper.

Kabocha Korokke

Pumpkin Croquettes

Kabocha, a pumpkin with edible green skin and bright orange flesh, makes a sweet, dense filling for korokke that kids (and my colleagues at work) like a lot. I form these croquettes into spheres the size of golf balls just because they cook quicker and they look cute! I stack them in a pyramid for an eye-catching presentation. For a main course, serve with shredded green cabbage or a green salad and bowls of rice and Miso Shiru (page 44). (For tips on deep-frying, see page 57.)

½ **kabocha** pumpkin, skin on, any seeds
    removed, and cut into 1- to 2-inch chunks
1 to 2 cups reduced-fat, low-sodium canned
    chicken broth or water
1 tablespoon unsalted butter
½ yellow onion, minced
2 tablespoons soy sauce
2 tablespoons mayonnaise

Pinch of salt
¼ teaspoon ground pepper
1 cup all-purpose flour
1 large egg
1 to 2 cups **panko** (page 18)
Canola or other neutral oil for deep-frying
Tonkatsu sauce (page 19) for serving

In a saucepan, combine the **kabocha** pieces with chicken broth to cover (using the broth rather than the water will contribute a little flavor; just be sure you use a low-sodium product). Place over medium heat, bring to a simmer, cover, and cook until the flesh and skin are soft enough to mash like potatoes, 15 to 20 minutes.

While the pumpkin is cooking, in a small frying pan, melt the butter over medium heat. When the butter is foaming, add the onion and cook, stirring often, until translucent, 4 to 5 minutes. Remove from the heat and set aside.

When the pumpkin is ready, drain well. The skin is edible, of course, but if you decide you don't want flecks of green in your **korokke**, you can let the chunks cool until they can be handled and then peel them, though the yield will be lower. (The skin is easier to peel after cooking than before.) I don't recommend peeling them, however, since the skin gets nearly as soft as the flesh and I like the green flecks. Transfer the pumpkin to a large bowl and, using a potato masher or the back of a fork, mash until fairly smooth, with just a few small chunks visible. Add the onion, soy sauce, mayonnaise, salt, and pepper and mix well. Let the mixture cool a bit before shaping and coating with the breading.

Spread the flour in a small, shallow bowl. Break the egg into a second shallow bowl and beat with chopsticks or a fork until well blended. Spread about 1 cup of the **panko** in a third shallow bowl. Spread a little **panko** on a flat plate or tray.

Dampen your hands with water and form the pumpkin mixture into about 20 golf ball–size balls. Gently dust each croquette with the flour, shaking off the excess; coat with the egg;

continued

and then coat with the panko, lightly pressing the panko in place with your fingertips. As each croquette is coated, set it aside on the panko-lined plate. As you work, add more panko to the bowl as needed. (At this point you can freeze the croquettes: arrange them on a platter or rimmed baking sheet, place in the freezer, and then transfer the frozen croquettes to a zippered plastic bag and return to the freezer for up to 3 months. You can deep-fry them directly from the freezer, but keep the oil temperature at 325° to 350°F and watch carefully to be sure the coating doesn't brown too quickly. I usually start the cooking at 350°F and then lower it if the coating is cooking too fast. The croquettes will still be very crispy, but the crumb coating will look flatter than the coating on fried freshly made croquettes.)

Pour the oil to a depth of 3 inches into a wok or deep, wide saucepan and heat to 350°F on a deep-frying thermometer or until a bit of panko dropped into the hot oil rises immediately to the top. Working in batches, drop the croquettes into the oil one at a time, being careful not to crowd the pan, and fry until medium brown and crispy, about 4 minutes. Using tongs or chopsticks, remove the croquettes from the oil and drain on a wire rack or on paper towels.

Serve the croquettes hot. Pass the tonkatsu sauce at the table for drizzling over or dipping the croquettes. Any leftovers can be eaten at room temperature for lunch the next day.

Makes about 20 small croquettes; serves 4 to 6 as an appetizer or 2 as a main course

Variation: If you like, you can add a little meat or poultry to the pumpkin mixture. In a small frying pan, heat 1 tablespoon canola or other neutral oil over medium heat. Add ¼ pound ground pork, chicken, or beef, sprinkle with 1 teaspoon sugar, and cook, stirring often and breaking up the meat with a wooden spatula or spoon, until it is no longer pink, 4 to 5 minutes. Sprinkle with 1 teaspoon soy sauce, mix well, and immediately remove from the heat. Add the cooked meat to the mashed pumpkin along with the onion.

Note: Sometimes kabocha can have very hard tan or brown calcified "warts" on the green skin. Although the skin is completely soft and edible when cooked, you should slice off these tan bits before cooking as they will not soften.

Otoosan no Kabocha Nimono

My Father-in-law's Sweet Simmered Pumpkin

In Tokyo in the summertime, it is traditional to go to watch the fireworks displays on the banks of the Tama River, which empties into Tokyo Bay. Thousands of people attend, and nearly everyone brings a picnic dinner. On one occasion, Shohei and I went with some newly married friends, and the wife proved the perfect hostess, first tying an apron around her waist and then serving us a delicious picnic supper, including a terrific kabocha nimono.

When my father-in-law found out that this was one of my favorite dishes, he offered to cook it for me. Everyone was amazed at his cooking skill, since seventy-five-year-old Japanese men are rarely found in front of a stove. Even my mother-in-law was impressed!

This side dish is typically found in a bento (boxed lunch), at a picnic, and on the dinner table but rarely in restaurants, and when it is cooked just right, it is sweet and savory and has a crumbly, floury, yet moist texture.

1 kabocha pumpkin, about 1 ¾ pounds
1¼ cups dashi or reduced-fat, low-sodium
    canned chicken or vegetable broth
1½ tablespoons mirin

1 tablespoon sugar
¼ teaspoon salt
¾ teaspoon soy sauce

Cut the kabocha in half and remove and discard the seeds. Using a vegetable peeler, remove random strips of the skin, so the pumpkin has a mottled appearance, leaving most of the skin intact. This will allow the cooking liquid to flavor the pumpkin better. Cut the pumpkin into 1½-by-2-inch chunks.

Place the pieces skin down in a deep frying pan. Measure the dashi in a measuring cup, add the mirin, sugar, salt, and soy sauce, stir well, and pour the mixture into the pan. The liquid should reach about halfway up the sides of the pieces. Cover with a drop-lid (page 22), bring to a boil over high heat, reduce the heat to medium-low, and simmer until the pumpkin is tender, 20 to 25 minutes.

Remove from the heat, take off the lid, and allow the pumpkin to sit in the cooking liquid that remains for 15 to 20 minutes. It will soak up most of the liquid. Serve warm or at room temperature.

Serves 6 to 8 as a side dish

Mapo Nasu

Spicy Chinese-Style Eggplant with Pork

The cooking sauce for this dish is the same one I use for making **Mapo Dofu** (page 28). The fried eggplant is crispy and creamy at the same time, and when combined with the rich sauce, the resulting marriage is perfect over a bowl of rice. Use slender, firm Japanese or Chinese eggplants to make this dish. You can adjust the level of spiciness to your own taste.

6 green onions
3 cloves garlic, minced
1-inch piece fresh ginger, peeled and minced

Sauce
2 teaspoons chili bean paste
½ cup reduced-fat, low-sodium canned
  chicken broth
1 teaspoon oyster sauce
1 tablespoon soy sauce
1 tablespoon sake

1 teaspoon sugar
2 teaspoons cornstarch dissolved in
  2 teaspoons water
About 1 teaspoon sesame oil (optional)

4 Japanese or Chinese eggplants, about
  1 pound total weight
6 tablespoons canola or other neutral oil
½ pound ground pork
2 to 3 cups hot cooked rice (see **Gohan**,
  page 140)

Mince the white parts and tender green tops of 4 green onions, then mince the white part only of the remaining 2 green onions. Cut the tender green tops of these last 2 onions in half lengthwise, and then cut crosswise into 1-inch lengths. Place the minced onion, garlic, and ginger in 3 small separate bowls. Set the green onion tops aside separately.

Ready the sauce ingredients. Measure the chili bean paste into a small bowl. In another small bowl, stir together the broth, oyster sauce, soy sauce, sake, and sugar. Set all the bowls near the stove. Have the cornstarch-water mixture and the bottle of sesame oil (if using) near the stove as well.

Trim the stem and blossom ends from the eggplants, and then cut in half lengthwise. Cut each half in half again lengthwise. Finally, cut each strip crosswise into ½-inch-thick pieces.

In a wok or large frying pan, heat 4 tablespoons of the canola oil over medium-high heat. When it is hot, add the eggplant pieces and stir-fry until soft, about 4 minutes. Transfer the eggplant to a bowl.

Wipe the pan clean and heat over high heat. When the pan is hot, add the remaining 2 tablespoons oil and swirl the pan to coat the bottom and sides. When the oil is very hot, add the garlic and cook, stirring constantly with a spatula so it does not burn, until fragrant. Then add the ginger and minced green onions, stir well, and reduce the heat to medium. Add the ground pork and continue to stir constantly, breaking up the pork and integrating it with the other ingredients. When the pork is just cooked, after about 2 minutes, add the chili bean paste and pour in the broth mixture. Using the spatula, combine all ingredients well with the sauce. Add the eggplant, stir well, and heat through. Stir the water-cornstarch mixture to recombine and then pour slowly into the pan and stir until the sauce thickens, about 1 minute more. Drizzle in a little sesame oil, if you like.

Spoon the eggplant-and-pork mixture into a serving bowl or onto a platter, family style, and serve each diner a bowl of rice. Or, spoon the mixture over individual bowls of rice. Garnish with the reserved green onion tops and serve.

Serves 4 as a main course

Deep-frying, Japanese Style

A number of terrific Japanese dishes call for deep-frying, which may surprise you—and which may put you off, too. Many cooks are afraid of deep-frying, viewing it as difficult and messy, and many eaters imagine that the food will be greasy. But frying can be both simple and neat if you follow a few easy rules, and Japanese deep-fried foods, correctly cooked, are never oily, but instead deliciously light and wonderfully crispy.

First, set up a workstation with the flour, egg, and *panko* you need for breading the food lined up in their order of use. Have a pair of long cooking chopsticks or tongs handy for getting the ingredients into and out of the hot oil safely and with a minimum of splashing. Or, you can use a slotted spoon or spatula for retrieving foods. A deep-fat fryer is a wonderful thing to have but it isn't essential; my mother-in-law doesn't have one and neither do I. A wok or a deep, wide saucepan works fine in its place. A deep-frying thermometer is a good tool for keeping track of the temperature of the oil. But if you don't have one, don't worry; I give an alternative test in every recipe. Also, here is a simple test that you can use whenever you are deep-frying: When you think the oil is hot, hold a wooden chopstick upright in it. If small bubbles form around the chopstick immediately, the oil is ready. A wire rack for draining the fried foods is ideal (paper towels are an easy alternative) and a small skimmer for scooping fried bits out of the oil—otherwise they will burn—is handy. Both are inexpensive.

Always cook foods in small batches. If you crowd the pan, the oil temperature will drop, causing the foods to absorb the oil. And after you remove a batch from the pan, be sure the oil returns to the correct temperature before you slip the next batch into the pan or, again, the foods will absorb the oil.

Now you know the easy rules, so you never need to have a fear of frying! Some of the most delicious dishes in the Japanese repertoire—especially *korokke* and *tonkatsu*—are not to be missed.

Nasu Dengaku

Eggplant with Miso Topping

Anyone who is on the fence about eggplant is sure to be converted by this dish. Dengaku is traditionally firm tofu threaded onto flat wooden skewers, topped with miso, and grilled. Here, eggplant is topped with a sweet, rich miso sauce and then broiled until the topping is bubbling and delectable. It is a great summer's night treat, cooked outdoors on a grill. I enjoyed it at a *yakitori* stand (page 115), along with many skewers of grilled chicken and a few *jokki* of beer. Draft beer is ordered by size, with a *chu jokki* used for medium and a *dai jokki* for large. After a couple of *dai jokki*, it's all you can do to get to the train that will carry you home.

Dengaku topping is delicious on eggplant as presented here, but it is also good on chicken, with the sauce ingredients in slightly different proportions (see *Toriniku no Misoyaki*, page 118).

Miso Topping
5 tablespoons white miso
2 ½ tablespoons sugar
1 tablespoon mirin
1 large egg yolk
½ cup water

4 Japanese or Chinese eggplants, about
    1 pound total weight
1 tablespoon sesame oil
1 tablespoon canola or other neutral oil
Sesame seeds, toasted (see page 20),
    for garnish

To make the miso topping, in a small saucepan, stir together the miso, sugar, mirin, egg yolk, and water. Place over medium-low heat and whisk constantly until the sugar is fully incorporated and the sauce is very smooth, about 4 minutes. Do not allow it to boil. Remove from the heat and set aside.

Trim off the stem and blossom ends from each eggplant. Cut each eggplant in half lengthwise, and score the cut sides with shallow 1/4-inch cross-hatching. This will help the miso topping stick to the eggplant.

Preheat the broiler. In a large frying pan, heat the sesame and canola oils over medium-high heat. When they are hot, add the eggplant halves, cut side down, to the pan. (If your pan is not large enough to accommodate all the eggplant halves, cook them in 2 batches, using half of the oil for each batch.) Cook until lightly browned, about 4 minutes. Then, using tongs, carefully turn and cook skin side down until the eggplants are soft but still hold their shape, about 4 minutes more. Adjust the heat if necessary to keep the eggplants from burning.

Transfer the eggplant halves, cut side up, to a broiler pan. Spread an equal amount of the miso topping over the top of each eggplant half. Slip the pan under the broiler about 4 inches from the heat source and broil until the miso topping just begins to brown, about 5 minutes. Remove from the broiler and garnish with the sesame seeds. Serve piping hot.

Serves 4 as an appetizer or side dish

Nasu no Agebitashi

Spicy Sweet-and-Sour Eggplant

I first had this addictive dish at the home of my husband's friend Shizuo Isomae and his wife, Kyoko. It was just one of the many little dishes Kyoko had made in her tiny kitchen for the dinner. I was so impressed that I had to have the recipe, but somehow I lost the paper on which I wrote it. I then discovered that it is a very popular **otsumami** (loosely translated, appetizer), and that my sister-in-law Emiko, also a terrific cook, had her own version, so I am including her recipe here.

If you have trouble locating chili bean paste, you can use any Asian chili paste that you like. If you can find only American or Italian globe eggplants, you can still make the recipe. Choose 4 eggplants that weigh about 1/2 pound each and cut them into pieces about 2 inches wide, 1 1/2 inches long, and 1/2 inch thick.

Canola or other neutral oil for deep-frying
8 Japanese or Chinese eggplants, about
    2 pounds total weight, trimmed and cut
    crosswise into 2-inch-thick pieces

1/4 cup mirin
1/4 cup soy sauce
1/4 cup rice vinegar
1 teaspoon chili bean paste
1 to 2 tablespoons sugar

Sauce
1 teaspoon minced garlic
1 tablespoon peeled and minced fresh ginger

3 tablespoons minced green onion, including
    tender green tops

Pour the canola oil to a depth of 3 inches into a wok or deep, wide saucepan and heat to 350°F on a deep-frying thermometer or until bubbles immediately form around a wooden chopstick held upright in the pan. Working in batches, add the eggplant pieces, being careful not to crowd the pan. Fry, turning as needed, until soft and lightly browned, 4 to 5 minutes. Using chopsticks or tongs, remove to a wire rack or paper towels to drain.

To make the sauce, in a small saucepan, stir together the garlic, ginger, mirin, soy sauce, vinegar, chili bean paste, and sugar and place over low heat. (I prefer the smaller amount of sugar, but you if like a little more sweetness, add the larger amount.) Cook, stirring constantly, until the sugar dissolves, about 2 minutes. Remove from the heat.

Pour the sauce into a serving bowl, add the eggplant, and mix lightly to coat all the eggplant with the sauce. Top with the green onions. Serve warm or at room temperature.

Serves 4 as an appetizer or side dish

Grilling, Japanese Style

Outdoor grilling is uncommon in Japan, as few homes have sufficient backyard space for the necessary equipment. Despite that, *yakimono*, or "grilled foods," have been popular for centuries and are among the most important elements of the national cuisine. Indeed, most meals include a grilled dish, usually fish and sometimes meat or vegetables, whether eating out or at home. Restaurants specializing in eel *kabayaki* are smoky places where succulent eel is continually basted in a sweet sauce as it cooks on large grills. At a *yakitori-ya*, grilled skewered chicken is the specialty, and all different parts of the bird, from the thigh meat to the hearts, are cooked. At *robata-yaki* and *teppan yaki* establishments, all kinds of foods—meats, seafood, vegetables—are cooked on a grill or on a griddle, respectively. Finally, there is the popular *yakiniku* (literally, "grilled meat") places, where customers grill their own meals.

With the right grill or griddle, all of these specialties can be cooked at home. Since in Japan this usually means cooking inside the house, the kitchen can get a bit smoky, and anyone lucky enough to have an outdoor space or a portable electric griddle will probably use it. Most Japanese kitchens, although lacking an oven, have a clever little grill that slides into a space under the kitchen counter. It is shallow, only eight to twelve inches, so the food stays close to the heat source. Unlike a broiler, the temperature is adjustable and the food rests on a rack, with a drip pan below. Filling the drip pan with water reduces the amount of smoke produced, and also the smell, and it helps to keep the food moist as it cooks. The result is food that tastes like it was grilled outdoors.

Because of the size of these indoor grills, flat foods are most easily cooked, with fish the most common, along with skewered chicken and sliced vegetables. A whole chicken or even chicken parts won't fit. An ear of corn, however, will fit and is one of the simplest and happiest surprises for its superb taste. In a Western kitchen, similar results can be achieved using a gas or charcoal grill outside, or even a standard oven broiler (see recipe, page 48).

Nasu no Soboro Ankake

Eggplant with Gingery Chicken Sauce

In this recipe, soft, rich, quickly fried eggplant is topped with a sweet and gingery ground chicken "gravy"—the same sauce that is paired with soft tofu on page 32. The dish looks and tastes like it is difficult to make, but it is actually easy enough for a weeknight dinner.

Quickly frying the eggplant in oil gives this dish richness without imparting an oily taste. Slender, dark purple Japanese eggplants (or their lavender Chinese counterparts) are wonderful because they have few seeds and are not as bitter as larger varieties. If you can find only American or Italian globe eggplants, choose one that weighs about 1 pound and cut it crosswise into 1/2-inch-thick rounds.

Sauce
3/4 pound ground chicken
1 cup plus 2 tablespoons water
2 tablespoons plus 3/4 teaspoon soy sauce
1 teaspoon ginger juice (see page 16)
1 teaspoon mirin
1 tablespoon plus 3/4 teaspoon sugar
1 tablespoon cornstarch dissolved in
   5 teaspoons water

4 Japanese or Chinese eggplants, about
   1 pound total weight
1/4 cup canola or other neutral oil
1 tablespoon soy sauce
1-inch piece fresh ginger, peeled, cut into
   fine slivers, and immersed in cold water
   to crisp

To make the sauce, in a saucepan, combine the chicken, water, 2 tablespoons plus 3/4 teaspoon soy sauce, ginger juice, mirin, and sugar and place over medium heat. Cook, stirring often and breaking up the chicken with a wooden spoon, until the chicken is no longer pink, about 5 minutes. Stir the water-cornstarch mixture to recombine and then pour slowly into the pan and stir until the sauce thickens, about 1 minute. Remove from the heat and set aside.

Trim off the stem and blossom ends from each eggplant. Cut each eggplant in half lengthwise and score the skin sides with shallow 1/4-inch cross-hatching.

In a large frying pan, heat the oil over medium-high heat. When the oil is hot, add the egg-plants, cut side down, to the pan. While you are not exactly deep-frying the eggplant, you want there to be sufficient oil for the eggplant to become crispy outside and soft inside. (If your pan is not large enough to accommodate all the eggplant halves, cook them in 2 batches, using half of the oil for each batch.) Cook until lightly browned, about 4 minutes. Then, using tongs, carefully turn and cook skin side down until the eggplants are soft, about 5 minutes more. Adjust the heat if necessary to keep the eggplants from burning. Remove the eggplants from the pan and sprinkle with the 1 tablespoon soy sauce.

continued

Just before the eggplants have finished cooking, gently reheat the sauce. Divide the eggplant halves, cross-hatched side up, between 2 shallow bowls and spoon the sauce over the top. Drain the ginger slivers and use to garnish each bowl. Serve immediately.

Serves 2 as a main course

Kabocha no Soboro Ankake (Pumpkin with Gingery Chicken Sauce) Variation: Kabocha pumpkin is also delicious topped with this gingery sauce. Remove the seeds from 1/2 kabocha pumpkin and cut the pumpkin into 1 1/2-inch chunks with the skin intact. Place in a steamer basket and steam over simmering water until tender, 15 to 20 minutes. Divide the pumpkin between 2 shallow bowls and top with the sauce. Serve immediately.

Yasai Itame

Stir-fried Vegetables with Pork

A crunchy mix of vegetables and savory bits of pork simply stir-fried over high heat, this is a great way to use up leftovers. My Japanese family is loath to waste food—a rule that is easy to obey if you have this popular dish in your repertoire. College kids cook it in their dorms and busy moms make it for their families. If you have a wok, all the better, but a frying pan is fine, too. The trick is to get the heat up as high as you can—the vegetables need to cook very quickly so that they get a little charred yet remain crisp.

Salt

1 large carrot, peeled, cut crosswise into thirds, and then thinly sliced lengthwise

6 slices thick-cut bacon, cut into 1-inch pieces

1 tablespoon canola or other neutral oil

½ green bell pepper, seeded, cut lengthwise into ¼-inch-wide strips, and strips halved crosswise

1 small yellow onion, cut into ¼-inch-thick slices

4 fresh shiitake mushrooms, stems discarded and sliced (optional)

½ head green cabbage, outer layer of leaves discarded and chopped into 1½- to 2-inch pieces

4 or 5 green onions, including tender green tops, cut into 2-inch lengths

½ cup bean sprouts, both ends trimmed (optional)

Ground pepper

½ teaspoon soy sauce

Fill a small saucepan with water and bring to a boil. Salt the water lightly, add the carrot, and blanch for 1 minute. Drain into a sieve and immediately hold under running cold water to halt the cooking. Set aside.

Heat a wok or large frying pan over high heat. Add the bacon and stir until cooked through but not at all crisp, about 4 minutes. Using a slotted spoon, transfer to a bowl and set aside.

Pour out any fat from the pan, wipe it clean, and return the pan to high heat. When the pan is hot, add the oil, swirl to coat the bottom and sides, and heat until the oil is almost smoking. Add the bell pepper, yellow onion, mushrooms (if using), and carrot and stir-fry for 2 to 3 minutes. Add the cabbage, green onions, and bean sprouts (if using) and stir-fry for 2 minutes longer. Return the bacon to the pan and stir-fry for 1 minute. At this point, all the vegetables should be just barely tender. Season to taste with salt and pepper, drizzle with the soy sauce, and remove from the heat.

Transfer to a large platter and serve immediately before the vegetables have a chance to get soggy.

Serves 4 as a main course

Mayumi no Roru Cabegi

Mayumi's Cabbage Rolls

I grew up with a Russian grandmother, so the stuffed cabbage I was used to eating was a tasty but heavy lump, filled with beef and rice, napped with a sweet-and-sour tomato sauce, and accompanied by a side of mashed potatoes. I couldn't move for days after I ate it. Mayumi, Shohei's sister, introduced me to this sappari (light) version, stuffed with pork and shrimp and served in chicken broth. Make the rolls on the smallish side, so they are easier to handle and cook quickly. While I love to eat the rolls hot in the soup in which they are cooked, they are also good at room temperature, sliced and drizzled with a little of the ketchup-and-mayonnaise sauce.

1 head green cabbage, outer layer of leaves discarded

5 green onions, including tender green tops, thinly sliced

2 slices white bread, torn into small pieces

1/4 pound shrimp, peeled, deveined, and chopped into small pieces

1/4 pound ground pork

1 1/2 teaspoons ginger juice (see page 16)

1/2 teaspoon salt, plus more for seasoning

1/4 teaspoon ground pepper

1 tablespoon sake

5 cups reduced-fat, low-sodium canned chicken broth

1/4 cup tomato ketchup

5 tablespoons mayonnaise

Fill a large pot three-fourths full of water and bring to a boil. Add the cabbage, submerging it in the water. When the water returns to a boil, remove the cabbage from the pot with tongs and place it in a colander to drain. Reserve 5 tablespoons of the boiling water for the sauce (you may not use all of it).

When the cabbage is cool enough to handle, carefully peel away the leaves without tearing them. As the leaves are removed, place them on paper towels to absorb the excess water. You will need 8 large leaves without rips, tears, or heavy spines. If you can salvage more leaves, do so, in case you have extra filling.

In a bowl, combine the green onions, bread, shrimp, pork, ginger juice, 1/2 teaspoon salt, pepper, and sake. Using your hands, mix the ingredients together until evenly distributed.

In a large saucepan, heat the chicken broth over medium-high heat. While the broth is heating, prepare the rolls: Position a leaf with the stem facing you. Place 2 to 3 tablespoons of the filling in the middle of the leaf, bring the edge nearest you over the filling to cover it, fold in both sides, and then roll up the leaf. Secure the roll with a toothpick, being careful not to tear the cabbage leaf. Repeat to make 7 more rolls.

At this point, the broth should be at a slow boil. Carefully add the cabbage rolls to the pan. They usually fit in a single layer, with just 1 or 2 rolls on top. Cover the pan with a drop-lid

continued

(page 22) and cook until the cabbage leaves are very tender but not disintegrating, 30 to 35 minutes. To test, prod a roll or two with a fork or chopstick; the leaf should be very easily pierced. Taste the broth and season with salt if needed.

In a small bowl, stir together the ketchup, 3 tablespoons of the reserved cabbage cooking water, and the mayonnaise until well combined. If you have ended up with extra filling and the leaves to wrap it, you will want the remaining 2 tablespoons water for mixing up extra sauce.

To serve, place 2 cabbage rolls in a shallow bowl, add broth to each bowl to reach about halfway up the sides of the rolls, and drizzle with the sauce. (Or, if you want to serve the rolls as appetizers, divide the rolls, broth, and sauce among 8 bowls.) Serve immediately.

Serves 4 as a main course or 8 as an appetizer

Kaneko no Uchi no Kenchin Jiru

The Kanekos' Hearty Japanese Vegetable Soup with Pork

Here is an example of Japanese cooking at its best: common ingredients, prepared simply but in a way that results in an extraordinary, soul-warming dish. This soup is among the best examples of **okaasan no ryori**—"mother's cooking"—and every mother has her own version. Although **kenchin jiru** is traditionally made with only vegetables, Shohei's mother uses a little fatty pork, known as **baraniku**, literally "belly meat," in hers, which I have substituted here with bacon. The soup is easily made vegetarian by omitting the bacon and adding another vegetable, such as a couple of leeks or a sweet potato.

6 slices thick-cut bacon, cut into 2-inch pieces

1 tablespoon canola or other neutral oil

2 small russet potatoes, peeled and cut into 1-inch chunks

6-inch piece daikon, about 3 inches in diameter, peeled, halved lengthwise, and then cut crosswise into ¼-inch-thick half-moons, or 10 red radishes, trimmed and cut into ¼-inch-thick slices

1 carrot, peeled, cut in half lengthwise, and then cut crosswise into ¼-inch-thick half-moons

1 parsnip, peeled, cut in half lengthwise, and then cut crosswise into ¼-inch-thick half-moons

5 or 6 fresh shiitake mushrooms, stems discarded and caps sliced ¼ inch thick

3 cups water

1 tablespoon dashi powder or granules or powdered chicken bouillon or 1 bouillon cube

¼ cup soy sauce, plus more as needed

2½ tablespoons mirin

1 tablespoon sugar

½ block soft, medium, or firm tofu, about 7 ounces

Salt (optional)

2 tablespoons minced green onion, including tender green tops

Ichimi togarashi or **shichimi togarashi** (page 20) for serving

In a frying pan, fry the bacon over medium-high heat until some of the fat starts to render but the bacon does not start to crisp, about 4 minutes. Using a slotted spoon, transfer the bacon to a stockpot or large saucepan. Discard the bacon fat.

Add the canola oil to the pot and place over medium-high heat. When the oil is hot, add the potatoes, daikon, carrot, parsnip, and mushrooms and cook, stirring often, for about 2 minutes. Add the water, dashi powder, ¼ cup soy sauce, mirin, and sugar and stir well. The liquid should cover the vegetables. Bring to a rapid simmer and reduce the heat to medium-low. Using your hands, break the tofu into 2-inch chunks and add them to the soup. Continue to cook, uncovered, over medium-low heat until the vegetables are soft, 30 to 40 minutes. If too much liquid seems to be evaporating before the vegetables are ready, cover the pot.

Taste and adjust the seasoning with salt or soy sauce. Ladle into warmed bowls and serve piping hot. Garnish each bowl with a little of the green onion and with **ichimi togarashi**.

Serves 2 as a main course or 4 as a first course

Yasai to Ebi Tempura

Vegetable and Shrimp Tempura

Tempura is of course popular in the West, so I had eaten it many times before my first visit to Japan. When I arrived in Tokyo, I discovered that, like teriyaki, tempura in its homeland is quite different from its Western counterpart. It seemed like all the tempura I had eaten in the United States was heavily battered, and I could finish only a few pieces before I was completely full. In Japan, where some of the finest restaurants specialize in the dish, I was introduced to tempura that was as light as air, had a melt-in-your mouth crispiness, and that I could eat and eat and eat without feeling stuffed.

The secret to good tempura lies in high-quality ingredients, a thin batter, and attentive frying. The batter itself is almost watery and lumps of flour are encouraged. If it is too well stirred, you will end up with a gummy, thick, floury coating that will absorb too much oil as it fries. The frying oil is usually safflower, sometimes with a touch of sesame oil, although I use canola oil with good results. You must use a large pot, keep the oil at a steady heat, fry no more than a few pieces at the same time, and constantly skim off any errant bits of batter from the oil. You will want to have all the foods you will be cooking ready to go before you start frying, and you should serve the tempura the moment it comes out of the hot oil. Diners can dip each piece into salt as they eat, or they can dunk each piece into a dipping sauce of dashi, mirin, soy, daikon, and ginger. The daikon is thought to aid in the digestion of oily foods, although if cooked correctly, your tempura will never be oily. (For tips on deep-frying, see page 57.)

Canola or other neutral oil for deep-frying
2 tablespoons sesame oil (optional)

Batter
1 or 2 trays ice cubes
1 cup all-purpose flour, sifted
1 cup ice water
1 large egg
Pinch of salt

4 to 8 large shrimp, peeled and deveined with tail segments intact
1 yellow onion, cut into 1/2-inch-thick slices
1/4 small **kabocha** pumpkin, skin on, any seeds removed and cut into 1/4-inch-thick slices

1 sweet potato, peeled and cut into 1/4-inch-thick slices
1 Japanese or Chinese eggplant, trimmed, halved crosswise, and then cut lengthwise into 1/4-inch-thick slices

Dipping Sauce
1 cup plus 1 tablespoon dashi or water
1/3 cup mirin
1/3 cup soy sauce

About 1/4 cup grated daikon (see page 15)
About 2 tablespoons peeled and grated fresh ginger

Pour the canola oil to a depth of 3 inches into a wok or deep, wide saucepan, add the sesame oil (if using), and heat to 350°F on a deep-frying thermometer or until bubbles immediately form around a wooden chopstick held upright in the pan.

While the oil is heating, make the batter. Fill a large bowl with the ice cubes, and then nest another bowl in the cubes. Add the flour, ice water, egg, and salt to the second bowl and, using a fork or chopsticks, stir lightly just until all the flour is moistened and the egg is incorporated. The batter should be lumpy, rather than smooth. Place near the stove.

Ready the shrimp, onion, pumpkin, sweet potato, and eggplant and place near the stove.

To make the dipping sauce, in a small saucepan, heat the dashi over medium-low heat. Add the mirin and soy sauce, stir to mix, remove from the heat, and keep warm. Have the daikon and ginger ready.

When the oil is ready, pick up 1 piece of any of the foods you will be frying and dip it briefly into the batter, being careful not to coat it too heavily, and carefully drop it into the hot oil. Repeat with just a few more pieces, and never crowd the pan. (Because you can cook only a few pieces in each batch, frying tempura can take a long time. But if you try to add more pieces to the oil, they will steam, rather become crisp.) As the foods fry, use a slotted spoon or wire skimmer to remove the little bits of batter floating in the oil. Fry until the coating is crispy but still light colored (not browned), 3 to 4 minutes for most foods. Pumpkin and sweet potato pieces might take a little longer, in which case you can lower the heat slightly so they do not color too much.

Using chopsticks or the slotted spoon or skimmer, transfer the pieces to a wire rack or paper towels to drain. Divide the warm dipping sauce between 2 small bowls and divide the daikon and ginger between 2 small plates. Serve the tempura immediately with the dipping sauce. Each diner mixes the daikon and ginger into their bowl of sauce to taste.

Serves 2 as a main course

Okaasan no Potato Sarada

My Mother-in-law's Potato Salad

I was surprised when potato salad showed up first in the bento (boxed lunch) I bought for lunch every day from the corner store, and then on my mother-in-law's dinner table. I was also relieved—finally something I recognized! Potato salad is a widely popular "adopted" side dish in modern Japanese cooking, always prepared with a Japanese twist of course. The additions of cucumber, apple, and ham in this recipe are typical of the universally accepted Japanese version of this Western classic, but variations exist throughout the country. This salad is a great side dish to Hamburg (page 131), Tonkatsu (page 101), and Ebi Furai (page 78), and would also be at home at your Western-style summer barbecue. The Japanese even use potato salad as a sandwich filling, spreading the soft white bread with butter first. Don't knock it until you've tried it! A garnish of tomatoes or strawberries on the salad delivers a wonderful burst of color—a true Japanese presentation—and tastes good, too.

4 russet potatoes, about 2 pounds total weight
Salt
½ large carrot, peeled, halved lengthwise, and then cut crosswise ¼-inch-thick half-moons
1 cup water
½ yellow onion, sliced paper-thin and then each slice cut into 3 pieces
½ large English cucumber, peeled, halved lengthwise, any errant seeds removed, cut crosswise into ¼-inch-thick half-moons, and then salted, drained, and squeezed dry (see page 15)

3 slices smoked or boiled ham, cut into small pieces
½ Granny Smith or other tart apple, peeled, cored, cut lengthwise into ½-inch-thick slices, and immediately immersed in water to which 1 tablespoon fresh lemon juice has been added to prevent darkening
½ to ⅔ cup mayonnaise
Freshly ground pepper
Cherry tomatoes or strawberries, stems removed and halved through the stem end, for garnish

In a large saucepan, combine the potatoes and 1 tablespoon salt with water to cover by 1 to 2 inches, place over high heat, and bring to a boil. Adjust the heat to maintain a gentle boil and cook the potatoes, uncovered, until a skewer or chopstick can easily pierce all the way through a potato, 30 to 45 minutes.

When the potatoes are ready, using tongs, remove them from the water. Then, hold the potatoes in a clean, dry kitchen towel and rub gently to peel away the skins. Place the peeled potatoes in a bowl, add 1 teaspoon salt, and mash roughly with the back of a fork, leaving some chunks.

In a small saucepan, combine the carrot and water, bring to a boil, and cook until tender but not mushy, about 4 minutes. Drain into a sieve and immediately hold under running cold water to halt the cooking.

In a large bowl, combine the carrot, onion, cucumber, and ham. Drain the apple and add to the bowl with $1/2$ cup of the mayonnaise and mix well. Add the potatoes (they should be close to room temperature at this point, but it is fine if they are still a little warm) and mix to distribute all the ingredients evenly. Do not overmix; you want the potatoes to have a texture that is between roughly mashed and a little chunky. Taste and adjust seasoning with salt and pepper and add a little more mayonnaise if the salad seems dry.

Garnish the salad with the cherry tomatoes, arranging them around the rim. Serve at room temperature.

Serves 8 as a side dish

Makaroni Sarada (Macaroni Salad) Variation: To make Japanese-style macaroni salad, substitute 2 cups cooked elbow macaroni for the potatoes. Because each piece of macaroni is smaller than the potato pieces, cut the carrot, onion, cucumber, and apple into smaller pieces for the salad.

Fish and Shellfish

In my little neighborhood in Tokyo, there were two major places to buy fish: the big supermarket, which boasted a huge assortment of beautiful fish and shellfish packaged neatly in cellophane, and the local **sakana-ya**, or fish shop, in this case a small storefront run by a fishmonger and his wife and with opening hours that I could never quite figure out. The **sakana-ya** carried a smaller selection of perfect fish, shellfish, and other items from the sea, presented in their natural state—shiny scales, bright eyes, fins and tails intact. I always headed to the fish shop in hopes that it would be open. The fishmonger would walk me through what was good that day, and tell me how to prepare it. He introduced me to things from the sea that I had never seen or heard of, let alone eaten before, and gave me tastes of the sashimi (the freshest raw fish) so that I could learn what I liked—and what I didn't. Sometimes I didn't like a particular flavor or texture, but for the most part, the unusual items were both revelatory and wonderful.

Because Japan is an island nation, seafood has always been a focus of the diet, and much of what is eaten is simply grilled or simmered in a light sauce of soy and mirin. When I lived there, I could cook fish or shellfish every day for a year and still not have tried everything. Since the same variety and quality are not available outside of Japan, I have included only the recipes that I have found are possible to re-create authentically in my kitchen in the United States. You won't find sashimi and sushi, two of the most popular ways fresh fish are eaten in Japan, because they are not often prepared at home, but you will find other easy and delicious dishes that call for the fish and shellfish that you can find at your local market. Both fresh and frozen high-quality shrimp are readily available, for example, which is part of the reason you'll find an abundance of shrimp recipes here. The other part of the reason is because my family likes shrimp.

left: *Ebi no Chiri So-su*, page 76

Ebi no Chiri So-su

Shrimp in Mild Tomato Chili Sauce

If you have kids, you'll want to try this dish first. I find my kids will eat nearly anything if ketchup is involved, but even adults with more sophisticated tastes will find that this seemingly unsophisticated dish has a complex flavor. In Japan, this is both a popular lunch-counter option and a home-style main course. Glass cases in **deparchika** (see page 87) typically display glistening bowls of **ebi no chiri so-su**. Undoubtedly they are prepared with the finest shrimp and probably the finest ketchup, too. At the other extreme, Japanese grocers sell a boxed mix to which you add shrimp and green onions, but I find it too sweet for my taste. Making this dish at home from scratch is just as easy, and you can control the levels of heat and sweet. If you want to increase your family's vegetable intake secretly and painlessly, throw in a cup of chopped green cabbage when you are cooking the onion.

¾ pound shrimp, peeled and deveined
1 tablespoon cornstarch
1 tablespoon dry sherry
1 large egg white
3 tablespoons tomato ketchup
½ teaspoon soy sauce
1½ teaspoons sake
1 teaspoon sugar

2 cups canola or other neutral oil
¼ yellow onion, minced
½ teaspoon minced garlic
2 tablespoons peeled and minced fresh ginger
1 to 2 teaspoons chili bean paste
2 green onions, including tender green tops, minced

In a small bowl, combine the shrimp, cornstarch, sherry, and egg white and stir to coat the shrimp evenly. Let stand at room temperature for 15 minutes. Meanwhile, in another small bowl, stir together the ketchup, soy sauce, sake, and sugar and stir until the sugar dissolves. Set the bowl near the stove.

In a wok or large frying pan, heat the oil over high heat. When it is hot, add the shrimp and stir with a wooden spatula until they are a little crispy, about 5 to 6 minutes. Using tongs or a slotted spoon, remove the shrimp and place in a bowl.

Pour out all but 2 teaspoons of the oil from the wok. Return the wok to medium heat and swirl to coat the bottom and sides with the oil. Add the yellow onion and cook for 1 minute. Add the garlic and ginger and stir-fry briefly, just until fragrant. Add the chili bean paste, stir well, and then stir in the ketchup mixture. Return the shrimp to the pan, raise the heat to high, and cook, stirring, until all the ingredients are well combined and the shrimp are coated with the sauce, 1 to 2 minutes longer.

Transfer the shrimp to a serving dish and top with the green onions. Serve immediately.

Serves 4

Photo on page 74

Asari no Sakamushi

Steamed Clams in Sake and Butter Broth

One of the best things about living in Northern California is the ability to get fresh fish and shellfish at the numerous (primarily Chinese) markets. If you have access to fresh clams, this is a quintessential Japanese dish. The most difficult part of this recipe is removing the sand from the clams. This dish is served in homes and turns up on izakaya (page 30) menus. The broth should be drunk after the clams have been eaten, which is why you want to make sure it is sand free.

1 pound small hard-shell clams in the shell such as Manila or small littleneck
Salt
2 tablespoons unsalted butter

2 cloves garlic, finely minced
2 cups sake
½ bunch fresh chives, thinly sliced

Wash the clams under cold running water. Fill a large, wide, deep bowl half full with cold water, add 1 tablespoon salt, and stir to dissolve. Place the clams in the bowl. The clams will be submerged in the water. Let stand for an hour or two, changing the water frequently and adding a little salt each time. Each time you pour out the water, check the amount of sand it contains. The time needed for the mollusks to purge all their sand varies, depending on the type of clam and where the clams were purchased. When the water is free of sand, drain the clams, rinse thoroughly in fresh water one more time, and drain again. Discard any clams that do not close to the touch.

In a Dutch oven or other large, heavy pot, melt 1 tablespoon of the butter. When the butter melts and stops foaming, add the garlic and the drained clams. Immediately add the sake, cover, and cook without lifting the lid until all the clams have opened, check after 5 minutes.

Uncover and discard any clams that failed to open. Add the remaining 1 tablespoon butter and stir to mix. Ladle the clams and their broth into bowls and garnish with the chives. Serve hot.

Serves 2

Ebi Furai

Crispy Fried Shrimp

Cooked in the same style as Tonkatsu (page 101) and often served at the same restaurants, this is the best fried shrimp you'll ever eat. The light **panko** coating produces incredible crispiness with no evidence of grease, and the shrimp fry quickly, so this is not a time-intensive meal. Whenever I cook this dish, I buy more shrimp than I need for that day, bread the extra shrimp, and then freeze them for a quick dinner on another day. I arrange the breaded shrimp on a flat plate or rimmed baking sheet, place them in the freezer, and then transfer the frozen shrimp to a zippered freezer bag. They will keep for a month or two. You can cook them directly from the freezer, using a slightly lower oil temperature and a slightly longer cooking time. They will not get as crisp as freshly breaded shrimp, but they will still be very good. (For tips on deep-frying, see page 57.)

If you can't find extra-large shrimp, use large or medium-large shrimp in their place, increasing the number to 16 to 20. Serve the shrimp with rice and a green salad.

12 extra-large shrimp, peeled and deveined
½ cup all-purpose flour
1 large egg
1 to 2 cups **panko** (page 18)

Canola or other neutral oil for deep-frying
Prepared tartar sauce (or ¼ cup mayonnaise mixed with 2 tablespoons tomato ketchup) or **tonkatsu** sauce (page 19)

To keep the shrimp from curling during frying, make 3 or 4 shallow horizontal cuts across the belly of each shrimp and then stretch it out, pulling lightly—don't pull it into pieces—until it is straight. Spread the flour in a small, shallow bowl. Break the egg into a second shallow bowl and beat with a fork or chopsticks until well blended. Spread about 1 cup **panko** in a third shallow bowl. Spread a little **panko** on a flat plate or tray.

To bread the shrimp, one at a time, lightly dust them with flour, coating evenly and shaking off the excess; dip them in the egg; and then finally roll in the **panko**. Using your fingertips, lightly press the **panko** in place. As each shrimp is ready, place it on the **panko**-lined plate. As you work, add more **panko** to the bowl as needed.

Pour the oil to a depth of 3 inches into a wok or deep, wide saucepan and heat to 350°F on a deep-frying thermometer or until a bit of **panko** dropped into the hot oil rises immediately to the top. Working in 3 or 4 batches, drop the shrimp into the oil one at a time and fry until medium to dark brown, about 3 minutes. Using chopsticks or tongs, remove the shrimp from the oil and drain on a wire rack or on paper towels.

Spoon the tartar sauce into a small bowl. Serve the shrimp immediately. Pass the sauce at the table.

Serves 4

continued

𝒦aki 𝒡urai (Crispy Fried Oysters) Variation: There was a great little lunch spot near my office in Tokyo that always had a kaki furai special on Thursdays—five gorgeous oysters, crispy on the outside, juicy on the inside. This is a re-creation of that perfect lunch. Buy 1 or more jars shucked fresh medium to large oysters; you want 20 oysters in all. Drain the oysters well and then bread and fry them as directed for the shrimp. Serve with shredded green cabbage and tomato wedges topped with your favorite salad dressing. Pass tartar sauce and/or tonkatsu sauce and lemon wedges at the table. Serves 4.

Sake Batayaki

Panfried Salmon with Butter and Soy Sauce

On most days, my mother-in-law heads to the fish market or supermarket and buys whatever fish looks good that day—and something always does. Because of this ready availability and the country's long tradition of eating fish, most Japanese consume fish in some form daily, whether grilled as a main course or in the dashi (made from dried bonito flakes) used for making soup.

Not surprisingly, my husband grew up eating only the best, and is therefore quite picky. In San Francisco, we are lucky to be able to find what we want at Japanese and Chinese markets and at the fish counters at some high-end supermarkets. I have found that in other areas, where a Western supermarket is the only option, good-tasting fresh salmon is one of the most reliable fish you can buy. Happily, it lends itself beautifully to this recipe, which is also known as munieru in Japan and is an adaptation of the French preparation à la meunière (dusted with flour and sautéed in butter). A tomato salad, steamed potatoes or rice, and green beans panfried in butter are good accompaniments.

4 salmon fillets, preferably skin on, each
    about 6 ounces and ¾ inch thick
½ teaspoon salt
1 cup all-purpose flour

1½ tablespoons unsalted butter
1 tablespoon canola or other neutral oil
2 teaspoons soy sauce

Rub your fingers over the fish fillets to check for pin bones, and remove any you find with needle-nose pliers or simply by pulling them free with your fingertips. Pat the fish fillets dry with paper towels, and sprinkle the fillets on both sides with the salt. Put the flour in a shallow bowl or on a piece of aluminum foil and spread into a shallow layer.

Place a large frying pan over medium heat. While the pan is heating, one at a time, place the salmon fillets on top of the flour and lightly and evenly dust on both sides, gently patting off the excess. As the fillets are dusted, set aside on a plate.

When the pan is hot, add the butter and oil. When the butter has melted and is foaming, add the salmon fillets, skin side down. (If your pan will hold only 2 fillets at a time, cook the fillets in 2 batches. Don't dust with flour until just before cooking, and use half the butter and oil for cooking each batch.) Cook the fillets until browned and the skin is crisped on the first side, 2 to 3 minutes. Carefully turn the fillets over and cook on the second side until browned and the center is opaque when tested with a small knife, 2 to 3 minutes longer.

Just before removing the fillets from the pan, drizzle them with the soy sauce and gently shake the pan to distribute it evenly. Transfer the fillets to individual plates and serve hot.

Serves 4

Sake to Mayonnaisu

Broiled Salmon with Mayonnaise

Shohei and I have been very lucky to have some wonderful Japanese babysitters for our two daughters, Nami and Aya, both of whom speak Japanese along with English (which makes my husband's parents happy). I've learned a lot from the babysitters, too, as they also prepare meals for the girls. This recipe is courtesy of Miyuki san, who managed her own household with her two small children, as well as my kids, the cleaning, the school schedules, and the cooking. She is a master of the quick-to-table, tasty meal, which this recipe epitomizes. The simplest of fish dishes, it is assembled and cooked in less than a half hour. Only a little mayonnaise is used, yet it really dresses up the fish. Serve the salmon with Miso Shiru (page 44), steamed broccoli, and rice, or, if you have as much energy as Miyuki, you can make a side dish of Sunomono (page 69).

4 salmon fillets, preferably skin on, each about 6 ounces and ¾ inch thick
Salt

4 tablespoons mayonnaise mixed with 1 teaspoon fresh lemon juice or ½ teaspoon rice vinegar

Rub your fingers over the fish fillets to check for pin bones, and remove any you find with needle-nose pliers or simply by pulling them free with your fingertips. Pat the salmon fillets dry and salt them generously on both sides. Arrange in a single layer in a shallow dish, cover, and refrigerate for at least 10 minutes or for up to 1 hour. (Letting the fish sit with the salt "cooks" the outer layer, allowing the saltiness to penetrate better than just sprinkling the fillets with salt and cooking them immediately.)

When you are ready to cook, preheat the broiler. Lightly butter a rimmed baking sheet.

Place the salmon fillets, skin side down, on the prepared baking sheet. Place in the broiler about 4 inches from the heat source and broil until lightly browned and bubbly, 6 to 8 minutes. Turn the fillets carefully—they have a tendency to stick and break—and broil on the second side until the skin is browned and crisp, about 4 minutes.

Remove the baking sheet from the broiler and top each fillet with 1 tablespoon of the mayonnaise, spreading it evenly (Or, if you have mayonnaise in a plastic squeeze bottle, you can squeeze it on in attractive squiggles.) Return the salmon to the broiler and broil until the mayonnaise is browned, about 2 minutes longer.

Transfer the fillets to individual plates and serve hot.

Serves 4

Kani Kurimu Korokke

Creamy Crab Croquettes

With a crispy outside and an interior of molten white sauce laced with crabmeat, this is a decadent and spectacular version of the *korokke* recipes (page 50) in the Vegetables chapter. Making the white sauce is straightforward, and the actual assembly of the croquettes is not difficult if you are careful to refrigerate the filling until it is well chilled and then work quickly to bread and fry. Believe me; this recipe is well worth the effort. Serve with Miso Shiru (page 44), a green salad or finely shredded green cabbage, and rice.

1 tablespoon unsalted butter
½ yellow onion, minced
¾ cup crabmeat (fresh or canned), picked
    over for shell fragments and cartilage
1 tablespoon white wine

White Sauce
3 tablespoons unsalted butter
¼ cup all-purpose flour

1½ cups whole milk
Pinch of salt

Canola or other neutral oil for deep-frying
½ to 1 cup all-purpose flour
1 large egg
1 to 2 cups **panko** (page 18)
Lemon wedges or ½ cup tomato ketchup
    diluted with ¼ cup hot water

In a small frying pan, melt the 1 tablespoon butter over medium-high heat. When the butter is foaming, add the onion and cook, stirring often, until translucent, 2 to 3 minutes. Add the crabmeat, stir to mix with the onion, and then add the wine. Cook for about 1 minute to evaporate any liquid and to cook off most of the alcohol from the wine. Remove from the heat and set aside.

To make the white sauce, in a saucepan, melt the 3 tablespoons butter over medium heat. When the butter is foaming, add the 1/4 cup flour in small increments and stir constantly to create a smooth paste, about 3 minutes. Do not allow it to color. Slowly add the milk to the flour paste, stirring constantly to prevent lumps from forming. Then cook, stirring constantly, until the mixture is thick and glossy, about 10 minutes. It should be about the consistency of mayonnaise. Add the salt, stir well, and then add the crab mixture and stir just until well combined.

Remove from the heat and spread the mixture in a cake pan, creating a layer about 1 inch thick. Let cool completely, then cover the pan with plastic wrap and refrigerate for at least several hours or for up to overnight. The mixture will solidify, making it easier to handle.

When ready to cook, pour the oil to a depth of 3 inches into a wok or a deep, wide saucepan and heat to 350°F on a deep-frying thermometer or until a bit of **panko** dropped into the hot oil rises immediately to the top.

While the oil is heating, spread the ½ cup flour in a small, shallow bowl. Break the egg into a second shallow bowl and beat with chopsticks or a fork until well blended. Spread about 1 cup **panko** in a third shallow bowl. Spread a little **panko** on a flat plate or tray.

Just before cooking, remove the crab mixture from the refrigerator. Using a metal spatula, divide the mixture into 8 equal portions. One at a time, using your hands and working quickly, form each portion into a small ball or oval. The less you touch the mixture, the easier it will be to work with. (The heat of your hands softens it.) Still working quickly, gently dust each croquette with the flour, shaking off the excess; coat with the egg; and then coat with the **panko**. Using your fingertips, lightly press the **panko** in place. As each croquette is ready, place it on the **panko**-lined plate. As you work, add more **panko** to the bowl as needed.

When the oil is ready, carefully drop 4 croquettes, one at a time, into the oil and fry until golden brown, 6 to 7 minutes. Using chopsticks if you are skillful, or a slotted spoon or spatula if you are not, carefully remove the croquettes (so they don't break open) and drain on a wire rack or on paper towels.

Serve the croquettes hot with the lemon wedges on the side. Or, spoon the sauce into a small bowl and pass at the table.

Makes 8 croquettes; serves 4

Corn Kurimu Korokke (Creamy Corn Croquettes) Variation: Substitute ¾ cup corn kernels, either fresh or well-drained thawed, frozen, for the crabmeat.

Buri no Teriyaki

Yellowtail Teriyaki

Teriyaki is a much misunderstood dish in the West. Order it here and more often than not you will be served a piece of broiled or panfried fish topped with a very sweet, sometimes gummy sauce. Usually there is far too much sauce for the poor piece of fish, too. Order teriyaki in Japan and you will be served a beautiful piece of grilled or panfried fish enhanced with— not overpowered by—a balanced sweet-and-salty glaze made from soy sauce, mirin, and sake. The glaze clings to the fish, rather than swamps it, flavoring it perfectly. You can make your own sauce or use one of Kikkoman's versions of teriyaki sauce in the same way. Just watch closely that the sauce doesn't burn too much. A caramelized burnish is the goal here. The same sauce can be used to create salmon teriyaki, chicken teriyaki, or beef teriyaki. Serve the fish with Miso Shiru (page 44), steamed or glazed vegetables, and rice.

4 yellowtail fillets, each about 6 ounces, 5 to 6 inches long, and about ¾ inch thick
¼ cup soy sauce
1 tablespoon sugar
1 tablespoon mirin
1½ teaspoons sake
1 tablespoon canola or other neutral oil

Rub your fingers over the fish fillets to check for pin bones, and remove any you find with needle-nose pliers or simply by pulling them free with your fingertips. Pat the fish fillets dry with paper towels. Arrange the fillets in a single layer in a shallow dish. In a small bowl, stir together the soy sauce, sugar, mirin, and sake until the sugar dissolves. Pour the mixture over the fillets, and turn the fillets to coat evenly. Cover and marinate in the refrigerator for 30 to 40 minutes.

In a large frying pan, heat the oil over medium heat. When the oil is hot, remove the fillets from the marinade, reserving the marinade, and add to the pan. Cook until medium brown on the first side, about 3 minutes. Carefully turn the fillets over and cook on the second side until light brown, about 2 minutes longer. Watch carefully that the glaze clinging to the fillets does not burn. If it seems like it might, reduce the heat to medium-low. Pour the reserved marinade over the fish and cook, gently shaking the pan initially to distribute the sauce evenly over the fish, until the sauce is reduced to a syrup and the fish is dark brown, 1 to 2 minutes longer.

Transfer the fish fillets to individual plates and serve hot.

Serves 4

Sake no Teriyaki (Salmon Teriyaki) Variation: Salmon fillets can be substituted for the yellowtail fillets.

Deparchika

The *deparchika*, or department-store basement floor, is a central element in the complex world of Japanese food. It is traditionally filled with individual "shops"—glass counters or mini food stalls—each one offering a different specialty, from tempura, sushi, and potato croquettes to German sausages, Korean kimchee, and Chinese noodles, plus there is always a big supermarket packed with fresh fish, meat, and vegetables. Famous restaurants often have small take-out operations featuring a signature dish, and bakery stands rival their street-address competition, with a wide array of desserts and sweets, both Japanese and Western (particularly French).

The quality of the prepared foods is universally exceptional, with prices to match. A tasting of some of them (usually the seaweeds, dried fish, pickled plums, and other bite-size delicacies, but not the items behind the counters) is offered freely, particularly to curious and adventurous (and, of course, polite) foreigners. Housewives rushed for time regularly purchase an entire meal in a *deparchika*: appetizer, main dish, side dishes, dessert, maybe a bottle of wine—a quick but pricey solution to a family dinner.

Ebi to Hotate no Doria

Shrimp and Scallops with Rice in a Creamy Casserole

One of the most interesting activities in Tokyo is shopping; the variety of the merchandise and the sheer number of stores are amazing. A single department store usually harbors dozens of individual boutiques and other freestanding shops, along with the **deparchika** (page 87), and at least one or two floors at the top of the store filled with small restaurants, each with its own specialty. Since shopping and eating are two things you can do with a minimal command of the language, I spent a good deal of time in these consumer emporiums. It was in one of these shopping palaces, sitting alongside other spent (mostly female) shoppers, that I first encountered this dish, another Japanese adoption of a Western dish. Seafood **doria** (I have never figured out the provenance of the name but the dish seems French-ish to me) is the most common version, but it can be prepared with meat and/or vegetables, too.

White Sauce
4 tablespoons unsalted butter
6 tablespoons all-purpose flour
2 cups whole milk
Pinch of salt

½ pound small shrimp, peeled
¼ pound sea scallops, cut into bite-size
    pieces
¼ cup white wine
1 tablespoon unsalted butter
½ yellow onion, minced

½ cup chopped fresh white mushrooms
½ teaspoon minced garlic
Pinch of salt
Pinch of ground pepper
2 cups cooked rice (see **Gohan**, page 140),
    warm or at room temperature

Topping
1 cup finely shredded mild white cheese such
    as Monterey Jack
1 tablespoon chopped fresh parsley

Preheat the oven to 350°F. Butter an 8-inch square (5-cup) baking dish.

To make the white sauce, in a small saucepan, melt the 4 tablespoons butter over medium heat. When the butter is foaming, add the flour in small increments and stir constantly to create a smooth paste, about 3 minutes. Do not allow it to color. Slowly add the milk to the flour mixture, stirring constantly to prevent lumps from forming. Then cook, stirring constantly, until the sauce thickly coats the back of a spoon, 5 to 7 minutes. Stir in the salt. Remove from the heat and keep warm.

In a small bowl, combine the shrimp, scallops, and wine and let stand at room temperature for 10 minutes.

In a frying pan, melt the 1 tablespoon butter over medium heat. When the butter is foaming, add the onion and cook, stirring often, until translucent, 4 to 5 minutes. Add the mushrooms and cook, stirring occasionally, for 1 minute. Add the shrimp, scallops, and wine and stir to coat with the onion. Add the garlic, salt, and pepper and cook, stirring occasionally, until the shrimp and scallops are just cooked through, about 5 minutes. Remove from the heat and drain any liquid from the pan into a 2-cup glass measuring cup. Set the shrimp-and-scallop mixture aside. Add enough of the white sauce to the measuring cup to total 2 cups. (This recipe may make more white sauce than you need. Leftover sauce can be stored flat in a freezer bag and used to thicken soups or stews, or to enrich macaroni and cheese.)

Put the cooked rice in the prepared baking dish. Top evenly with the shrimp-and-scallop mixture, and then pour the white sauce evenly over the top so that the rice and shrimp-and-scallop mixture are just covered. Sprinkle the cheese evenly over the sauce.

Bake the casserole until the sauce is bubbling and the cheese is melted, 10 to 12 minutes. Sprinkle with the parsley and serve hot directly from the dish.

Serves 4

Ebi to Broccoli "Gratin"

Creamy Macaroni and Cheese with Shrimp and Broccoli

You probably didn't expect to find macaroni and cheese in a book devoted to Japanese home cooking. But this dish is a perfect example of the popularity of "borrowed" cuisine in Japan, and you will find it served in coffee shops, in fine hotels, and at home. In Japan, a gratin can have a wide variety of additions, from kabocha pumpkin, cauliflower, or potato to fish, meat, or shellfish. For example, small hard-shell clams and sliced pork are common ingredients. Here, I have added shrimp and broccoli. If you are using harder vegetables, such as kabocha, cauliflower, or potato, you need to cut them into relatively small pieces and cook them in a tablespoon or so of butter until they are just on the firm side of tender before you add them to the gratin.

White Sauce
4 tablespoons unsalted butter
6 tablespoons all-purpose flour
2 cups whole milk
Pinch of salt
1/4 cup finely shredded mild white cheese such as Monterey Jack

1/2 pound small shrimp, peeled
1/4 cup white wine
1 tablespoon unsalted butter
1/2 yellow onion, minced
1 cup small broccoli florets
1/2 teaspoon minced garlic

Pinch of salt
Pinch of ground pepper
2 cups cooked elbow macaroni, warm or at room temperature

Topping
1 cup finely shredded mild white cheese such as Monterey Jack
2 tablespoons panko (page 18) or plain bread crumbs
1 tablespoon unsalted butter, cut into small pieces
1 tablespoon chopped fresh parsley

Preheat the oven to 350°F. Butter an 8-inch square (5-cup) flameproof baking dish.

To make the white sauce, in a small saucepan, melt the 4 tablespoons butter over medium heat. When the butter is foaming, add the flour in small increments and stir constantly to create a smooth paste, about 3 minutes. Do not allow it to color. Slowly add the milk to the flour mixture, stirring constantly to prevent lumps from forming. Then cook, stirring constantly, until the sauce thickly coats the back of a spoon, 5 to 7 minutes. Add the salt and the 1/4 cup cheese, stir to melt the cheese, remove from the heat, and keep warm.

In a small bowl, combine the shrimp and wine and let stand at room temperature for 10 minutes. In a frying pan, melt the 1 tablespoon butter over medium heat. When the butter is foaming, add the onion and cook, stirring often, until translucent, 4 to 5 minutes. Add the broccoli and

continued

the shrimp and wine and stir to coat with the onion. Add the garlic, salt, and pepper and cook, stirring occasionally, until the shrimp turn pink and are just cooked through, 3 to 5 minutes. Remove from the heat and drain any liquid from the pan into a 2-cup glass measuring cup. Set the shrimp-and-broccoli mixture aside. Add enough of the white sauce to the measuring cup to total 2 cups. (This recipe may make more white sauce than you need. Leftover sauce can be stored flat in a freezer bag and used to thicken soups or stews, or to enrich macaroni and cheese.)

Put the cooked macaroni in the prepared baking dish. Spread the shrimp mixture evenly over the macaroni, and then pour the sauce evenly over the top so that the macaroni and shrimp mixture are evenly covered. Sprinkle the 1 cup cheese and then the *panko* evenly over the sauce and dot with the butter pieces.

Bake the gratin until the sauce is bubbling and the cheese has melted, 10 to 12 minutes. Turn the oven dial to broil, place the baking dish about 4 inches from the heat source, and broil until the top browns lightly, 1 to 2 minutes. Watch carefully to avoid burning.

Remove from the broiler, sprinkle with the parsley, and serve hot directly from the dish.

Serves 4

Menjo no Ebi Pirahu

Shrimp Pilaf, Japanese Style

Here is another Western-style dish that is served in hotel and department-store restaurants to "ladies who lunch," but is also popular with college kids who frequent coffee shops, where they catch up on the latest **manga** (serial comic books) while waiting for their meal to be served. Viewed as sophisticated French cuisine, perhaps this buttery rice dish has been embraced by the Japanese in part because it harks back to a traditional Japanese pilaf called **maze gohan** (mixed rice) that is virtually fat free and includes mushrooms and various other nutritious vegetables. To heck with that! This pilaf is easy to prepare and keeps well refrigerated or frozen, making it ideal for home kitchens. I got the recipe from one of my husband's colleagues, Hiroshi Menjo, whose wife, Ellie, is an amazing cook, but who also apparently has some tricks up his own sleeve!

¾ pound shrimp, peeled and deveined
1 tablespoon white wine
1 teaspoon plus 1 tablespoon canola or other neutral oil
4 tablespoons unsalted butter
½ large yellow onion, minced
2 cups sliced fresh white mushrooms

½ teaspoon salt
Ground pepper
2 cups cooked rice (see **Gohan**, page 140), at room temperature or cold
Pinch of paprika
2 tablespoons grated Parmesan cheese
2 tablespoons chopped fresh parsley

Preheat the oven to 375°F. Butter an 8-inch square (5-cup) baking dish.

In a bowl, combine the shrimp and wine and let stand at room temperature for 10 minutes.

In a large frying pan, heat the 1 teaspoon oil and the butter over medium heat. When the butter is foaming, add the onion and cook, stirring often, until translucent, 4 to 5 minutes. Add the mushrooms and cook, stirring occasionally, for 1 minute, and then add the shrimp and wine and stir to coat with the onion. Cook, stirring occasionally, until the shrimp turn pink and are just cooked through, 3 to 5 minutes; the timing will depend on the size of the shrimp. Add the salt and pepper to taste and then transfer the shrimp mixture to a large bowl.

Wipe the pan clean, return it to high heat, and add the 1 tablespoon oil. When the oil is almost smoking, add the rice and fry, stirring constantly, until the kernels are quite dry, about 5 minutes. Add the shrimp mixture, mix thoroughly, and reduce the heat to medium. Add the paprika, mix well, and transfer the mixture to the prepared baking dish. Sprinkle the cheese evenly over the top.

Bake the casserole for about 15 minutes. The mixture will dry a bit but will not look much different. Sprinkle with the parsley and serve immediately directly from the dish.

Serves 4

Meat and Poultry

Before I lived in Japan, I thought it was going to be fish, fish, fish, fish once I did get there. I figured that there would be some vegetables and, of course, rice. And I did encounter plenty of fish. But to my surprise—and delight—the moment I started eating what regular people eat and began cooking more and more with my mother-in-law and my sisters-in-law, I found that I was eating some kind of meat daily, usually chicken or pork but also beef.

Although beef was not a part of the Japanese diet until the arrival of the Meiji period in 1868, poultry and pork have a long history on the Japanese table. Japan is a small country, with little grazing land for cattle, so meat has been traditionally thought of as an expensive, hard-to-get ingredient. Now that Japanese tastes have expanded to include some Western dishes, meat and poultry are playing a much larger role in everyday cooking.

I came to Japanese cooking familiar with preparing meat, so discovering these meat recipes made me think that successfully cooking home-style Japanese dishes was actually possible. The recipes in this chapter might be the ones that surprise you the most, just as they did me. Hamburger, steak, fried chicken—are they really Japanese? Absolutely. If you are nervous at all about cooking and eating Japanese food, you might want to start here.

left: *Butaniku no Shogayaki*, page 96

Butaniku no Shogayaki

Panfried Ginger Pork

Juicy, gingery, and a little sweet, this is a great lunch or dinner main course that comes together quickly. I first encountered this *shogayaki* preparation at my local Tokyo convenience store late one night after work. The thinly sliced pork was presented with rice and a salad in a plastic box, and I don't know if it was the late hour or the quality of the convenience-store fare, but it became an instant favorite. I found premarinated meat at my local grocery and began making it myself. I eventually asked my mother-in-law for a from-scratch recipe, which proved to be so easy that I didn't need to buy it premade or premarinated ever again. The pork, rice, perhaps a steamed vegetable, and a little tomato or green salad are great in a lunch box or on the dinner table.

1 pound boneless pork loin chops

Marinade and Cooking Sauce
2 teaspoons ginger juice (page 16)
3 tablespoons sake

1½ tablespoons mirin
4½ tablespoons soy sauce

1½ teaspoons sesame oil
1½ teaspoons canola or other neutral oil

Cut the meat into about 12 slices, each 2 by 3 inches and 1/8 inch thick (see note). Set aside.

To make the marinade, in a bowl, combine the ginger juice, sake, mirin, and soy sauce and stir well. Add the pork, making sure that each piece is coated with the marinade. Let stand for 5 minutes, then turn the meat over in the bowl. Continue to marinate for at least 5 minutes longer but no more than 30 minutes or the meat will become hard.

Place a large frying pan over medium-high heat. When the pan is hot, add the sesame and canola oils and swirl the pan to coat the bottom and sides with the oils. When they are hot, remove the pork slices from the marinade and add them to the pan in a single layer. Pour the marinade over the pork. (If your pan is not large enough to accommodate all the pork, cook it in 2 batches, dividing the oil and marinade in half.) Cook the pork, gently shaking the pan occasionally to distribute the sauce, until browned on the first side, about 3 minutes. Then turn the pork pieces over and continue to cook until the second side is browned but the pork is still juicy, about 3 minutes longer.

Remove the pork from the heat and serve immediately.

Serves 3 or 4

Note: In Japan, grocers sell very thinly sliced pork tenderloin or loin. The easiest way to cut the meat yourself is to put the pork in the freezer for about 1 hour before you try to slice it.

Photo on page 94

Buta Tonjiru

Hearty Miso Soup with Pork and Vegetables

In the small town where I first lived in Japan, there was a great little restaurant that specialized in all kinds of pork dishes. I couldn't read the menu, so the waitress (also the owner) simply brought over their most popular dish, **tonjiru**. In Japan, pork belly (**baraniku**) is used for this soup, but you can use the thinly sliced meat of country-style pork ribs or thick-cut bacon slices. I have substituted a parsnip for the hard-to-find **gobo** (burdock in English), a long, slender root vegetable.

1 pound boneless country-style pork rib meat, cut into pieces 2 inches long by 1 inch wide by ½ inch thick, or thick-cut bacon, cut into 2-inch pieces

2½ quarts water

1-inch piece ginger, unpeeled, cut into 4 pieces

½ small daikon, peeled, cut into ¼-inch-thick slices, and the slices halved, or 10 red radishes, peeled and quartered

1 parsnip, peeled, halved lengthwise, and then cut crosswise into ½-inch-thick half-moons

1 carrot, peeled, halved lengthwise, and then cut crosswise into ½-inch-thick half-moons

1 russet potato, peeled and cut into 1½-inch chunks

½ cup miso, preferably red

1 tablespoon mirin

6 fresh shiitake mushrooms, stems discarded and caps cut in half

4 green onions, including tender green tops, cut on the diagonal into ½-inch pieces

Shichimi togarashi or equal parts black and cayenne or **ichimi** pepper (page 20)

If you are using the bacon, in a large frying pan, fry the bacon over medium-high heat until some of the fat starts to render but the bacon does not start to crisp, about 4 minutes. Using a slotted spoon, transfer the bacon to paper towels and pat to absorb the excess fat.

In a large saucepan, combine the pork rib meat or bacon, the water, and the ginger and bring to a boil over high heat. Skim off any foam that rises to the surface. Cover partially, reduce the heat to medium, and simmer for about 1 hour. Simmering it this long creates a flavorful broth. Remove the ginger from the saucepan and add the daikon, parsnip, and carrot to the broth, re-cover partially, and simmer over medium heat for 15 minutes. Add the potato, re-cover, and simmer for 10 minutes. Put ¼ cup of the miso into a small bowl, add a few spoonfuls of the soup broth, and stir with a fork or chopsticks until smooth. Reduce the heat to low, add the diluted miso to the pan, stir well, cover, and cook for 20 minutes. Do not allow the soup to come to a boil.

Put the remaining ¼ cup miso in the small bowl, dilute with the mirin and a few spoonfuls of the soup broth in the same way, and add to the pan along with the mushrooms. Re-cover and continue to cook over low heat until all the vegetables are very tender, about 15 minutes longer. Stir in the green onions and immediately remove from the heat. Ladle into warmed bowls and serve. Pass the **shichimi togarashi** at the table for diners to add to taste.

Serves 6

Kabu to Niku Dango

Hearty Meatball and Turnip Soup

I adapted this recipe for the Western kitchen from a recipe I saw in one of my favorite Japanese magazines for housewives, *Orenji Paji* (Orange Page). A weekly, the magazine is bright and colorful and carries lots of recipe ideas and cooking, cleaning, health, and relationship tips. Every week there is a different food focus, such as rice dishes, side dishes, foods that men like, and so on. This cross between a soup and a stew is a delicious way to use a vegetable that I seldom used before I started cooking Japanese food. You could use new potatoes in place of the turnips if you are turnip averse, although I think you will be happily surprised when you try them in this dish. The recipe is also very Japanese in its lack of waste—even the turnip tops are used.

Meatballs
½ pound ground beef
½ pound ground pork
1 teaspoon peeled and minced fresh ginger
1 green onion, including tender green tops, minced
¼ cup **panko** (page 18)
2 tablespoons sake
2 tablespoons water
2 teaspoons white miso
¼ teaspoon salt

Broth
3 cups dashi or reduced-fat, low-sodium canned chicken broth
2½ tablespoons soy sauce
2½ tablespoons sake
1 tablespoon mirin

6 small white turnips with green tops intact, turnips peeled and halved and tops trimmed and cut into 1-inch lengths

Salt
Ground pepper

To make the meatballs, in a bowl, combine the beef, pork, ginger, green onion, **panko**, sake, water, miso, and salt. Using your hands, mix the ingredients together until evenly distributed. Then, moisten your hands and shape the mixture into 1½-inch balls. You should have about 24 meatballs. Set aside.

To make the broth, in a large saucepan, combine the dashi, soy sauce, sake, and mirin and bring to a boil over high heat. Reduce the heat to medium, add the turnips, and cook for about 5 minutes. Add the meatballs and turnip tops, cover partially, and cook until the meatballs are cooked through and the turnips and turnip tops are tender, about 15 minutes longer. Season to taste with salt and pepper.

Divide the soup evenly among 4 warmed bowls, giving each diner 3 turnip halves and about 6 meatballs. Serve immediately.

Serves 4 as a main course

Subuta

Japanese-Style Sweet-and-Sour Pork

I ate this dish often in the little lunch place near my office in Tokyo, and I always watched the cooks behind the counter make it, hoping to learn the skill necessary to prepare it myself. It has a tangier taste and is not as heavily fried as the Westernized version of the same dish, and it is an ideal quick and tasty home-cooked main course. I've seen even quicker-cooking versions made with thinly sliced pork coated in cornstarch and sautéed instead of deep-fried. My family likes the dish made with larger pieces of pork, which is what I have done here.

1 carrot, peeled, halved lengthwise, and then cut crosswise into ½-inch-thick half-moons

Canola or other neutral oil for deep-frying, plus 3 tablespoons

1 pound pork tenderloin, cut into 1- to 1½-inch cubes

2 teaspoons soy sauce

1 teaspoon sake

¼ cup cornstarch

Sauce

1 tablespoon cornstarch

2 tablespoons water

¼ cup tomato ketchup

¼ cup sugar

¼ cup rice vinegar

1 teaspoon salt

1 teaspoon sesame oil

1 cup reduced-fat, low-sodium canned chicken broth

6 fresh shiitake mushrooms, stems discarded and caps halved if medium sized or quartered if large

1 yellow onion, halved through the stem end and cut into ½-inch-thick slices

½ large green bell pepper, seeded, cut lengthwise into 1-inch-wide strips, and strips halved crosswise

¼ cup sliced bamboo shoots

Fill a small saucepan with water and bring to a boil. Add the carrot and blanch for 1 minute. Drain into a sieve and immediately hold under running cold water to halt the cooking. Set aside.

Pour the oil to a depth of 3 inches into a wok or deep, wide saucepan and heat to 350°F on a deep-frying thermometer or until bubbles immediately form around a wooden chopstick held upright in the pan.

While the oil is heating, in a bowl, combine the pork, soy sauce, and sake and mix until the pork is evenly coated. Place the ¼ cup cornstarch in a small, shallow bowl near the stove.

When the oil is ready, dust a pork cube with the cornstarch, shaking off the excess, and drop it into the hot oil. Repeat with the remaining cubes, adding them one at a time. If you are using a wok, you should be able to fry all the pieces at once. If your pan is smaller, fry the pork cubes in batches. Fry the pork cubes, turning them often, until they are golden brown,

continued

about 5 minutes. Using a slotted spoon, transfer to a wire rack or paper towels to drain. To make the sauce, in a small bowl, stir together the 1 tablespoon cornstarch and water, mixing well. Place near the stove. In another bowl, combine the ketchup, sugar, vinegar, salt, sesame oil, and chicken broth, stir to mix well, and place near the stove.

Discard the oil in the wok and return the pan to medium-high heat. Or, if you don't have a wok, place a large frying pan over high heat. When the pan is hot, add the 3 tablespoons oil and swirl the pan to coat the bottom and sides. When the oil is hot, add the shiitake mushrooms and stir-fry briefly. Add the onion and bell pepper and stir-fry until the onion starts to turn translucent, 3 to 4 minutes. Add the carrot, bamboo shoots, and pork and stir-fry until well combined, about 1 minute. Pour in the ketchup mixture and mix well to combine all the ingredients with the sauce. Stir the water-cornstarch mixture to recombine and then pour slowly into the pan and stir until the sauce thickens and is glossy, 1 to 2 minutes.

Transfer the pork to a serving bowl or platter and serve immediately.

Serves 4

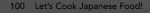

Tonkatsu

Crispy Fried Pork Cutlets

Rengatei, a Tokyo restaurant that opened in 1895, is credited with cooking Japan's first tonkatsu in 1899, and the fried pork cutlet has been popular throughout the archipelago ever since. Quickly deep-frying the lean pork—loin or tenderloin—at a high temperature and then carefully draining it results in a crispy, nongreasy, absolutely spectacular dish. Whenever I go to Japan, I have a list in my head of the things I want to eat, and tonkatsu is right at the top.

In Japan, restaurants specializing in tonkatsu offer the customer a variety of pork cuts, including hire (lean cut), rosu (fattier cut), and kurobuta ("black pig," pork from prized pure-bred Berkshire pigs). These specialty restaurants also usually offer kushi-katsu, chunks of rosu and onion that are breaded, skewered, and fried, as well as breaded and fried chicken (see variation), oysters (page 80), and shrimp (page 78). Tonkatsu is nearly always accompanied by a spicy, sweet, vinegary sauce with the strong taste of Worcestershire sauce. The recipes for house-made versions are usually closely guarded and a source of great pride. Happily, good-quality bottled tonkatsu sauce is now easy to find in the West, or you can substitute a few dashes of Worcestershire sauce or steak sauce. A large heap of finely shredded, crisp green cabbage is served alongside the pork, presumably to cut the fat. One popular Tokyo restaurant has waiters roving the floor with baskets full of freshly shredded cabbage to replenish diners' plates.

Cutlets

4 boneless pork loin chops, each about
    ¼ pound and ½ to ¾ inch thick
Canola or other neutral oil for deep-frying
1 to 2 cups all-purpose flour
1 large egg
3 to 4 cups panko (page 18)
1 teaspoon salt

Tonkatsu sauce (page 19)
Karashi (page 16) (optional)
½ head green cabbage, finely shredded
2 tomatoes, cored and quartered

If your pork chops are on the thick side (³/₄ inch), use a sharp knife to score one side lightly, making the cuts about 1 inch apart. This will ensure that thicker chops cook through.

Pour the oil to a depth of 3 inches into a wok or deep, wide saucepan and heat to 350°F on a deep-frying thermometer or until a bit of panko dropped into the hot oil rises immediately to the top.

While the oil is heating, spread the flour in a small, shallow bowl. Break the egg into a second shallow bowl and beat with chopsticks or a fork until well blended. Spread 3 cups of the panko in a third shallow bowl. Sprinkle a little panko on a flat plate or tray.

continued

To bread the cutlets, one at a time, sprinkle both sides of the cutlets with the salt. Dust them with the flour, shaking off the excess; coat with the egg; and then coat with the panko. Using your fingertips, lightly press the panko in place. As each cutlet is ready, place it on the prepared plate. As you work, add more panko to the bowl as needed.

When the oil is ready, add 1 or 2 breaded cutlets (it is imperative not to crowd the pan) and fry, turning often, until very crispy and medium-dark brown, about 6 minutes. Using tongs, transfer to a wire rack or paper towels to drain. Repeat until all the cutlets have been fried.

To serve, cut each chop crosswise into narrow strips and then reassemble the chops on 4 individual plates. Drizzle the tonkatsu sauce over the top and place a dab of karashi (if using) on the side. Serve the cabbage and tomatoes alongside.

Serves 4

Chikin Katsu (Crispy Fried Chicken Breasts) Variation: Substitute boneless, skinless chicken breasts for the pork and coat and fry the same way, but reduce the frying time to 4 to 5 minutes.

Katsudon (Pork Cutlet and Egg over Rice) Variation: A great way to use leftover (if there is any!) tonkatsu is in another popular favorite, katsudon, a variation of oyakodon (page 144). Fry 2 tonkatsu as directed and cut into bite-sized strips. Combine 1 tablespoon sake, 3 tablespoons soy sauce, 2 tablespoons mirin, 1 1/2 tablespoons sugar, and 1 cup reduced-fat, low-sodium chicken broth in a shallow frying pan, bring to a brisk simmer, and add 1/2 cup thinly sliced yellow onion. Cook until the onion is soft, about 5 minutes. Add 2 beaten eggs to the pan, cover, and cook until just set. Add the pork and 2 more beaten eggs, cover, and cook briefly (about 1 minute), then divide evenly between 2 bowls of rice.

Kurimu Shitu

Creamy White Chicken and Vegetable Stew

When I lived in Japan, I watched a lot of television in the hope that I would pick up the language better. Unfortunately, Japanese is not a language that you can just "pick up," but I did see a lot of food shows and did learn a lot of pop music. The commercials were the easiest "programs" for me to understand, and I would frequently see an ad for some kind of instant curry, stew, or other dish, and try to find it in the supermarket to prepare at home. Of course, the food you see advertised on television (in any country) is not always the healthiest, so I acquired a good knowledge of the convenience foods available in Japan.

One of the most enticing ads was for a white, creamy dish of meat and vegetables called **kurimu shitu**—"cream stew" to you and me. I am sure it is based on some imported dish, but I never figured out what the original was. I did try the boxed mix (kind of gummy), and then cooked it from scratch. Rich, creamy, full of meat and vegetables, and not any more difficult to prepare than the boxed mix, I found out why cream stew is so popular in Japanese homes. Because cooks in the United States don't have access to instant white sauce (a common staple in Japanese markets), you will have to make the sauce, but even that is surprisingly quick and easy. Serve the stew with a lettuce and tomato salad.

1 tablespoon unsalted butter

½ large yellow onion, minced

2 small russet potatoes, peeled, cut into 1½-inch pieces, and immediately immersed in water to which 1 tablespoon rice vinegar or white vinegar has been added to prevent darkening

1 cup fresh white mushrooms, stem ends trimmed and sliced

2 carrots, peeled and cut on the diagonal into ¼-inch-thick slices

1 pound boneless, skinless chicken thighs, excess fat removed and cut into bite-size pieces

3 tablespoons white wine

1½ cups reduced-fat, low-sodium canned chicken broth

1 bay leaf

1 cup broccoli florets

White Sauce

2 tablespoons unsalted butter

2 tablespoons all-purpose flour

1½ cups whole milk

½ cup half-and-half or heavy cream

Salt

Ground pepper

In a large, deep pot, melt the 1 tablespoon butter over medium-high heat. When the butter is foaming, add the onion and cook, stirring, until light brown, 5 to 7 minutes. Drain the potatoes, add to the pot along with the mushrooms, carrots, and chicken, and stir to mix. Add the wine, cook for 1 minute to cook off most of the alcohol, and then add the broth and bay leaf. When the broth comes to a gentle boil, reduce the heat to medium-low, cover partially, and cook until the chicken is cooked through and potatoes and carrots are tender, about 30 minutes.

While the stew is cooking, fill a small bowl with ice water and set aside. Bring a small saucepan filled with water to a boil. Add the broccoli and blanch for 1 minute. Drain and immerse immediately in the ice-water bath. Drain and set aside. (This step keeps the broccoli bright green.)

To make the white sauce, in a small saucepan, melt the 2 tablespoons butter over medium heat. When the butter is foaming, add the flour in small increments and stir constantly to create a smooth paste, about 3 minutes. Do not allow it to color. Measure the milk and cream in a measuring cup and slowly add the milk mixture to the flour paste, stirring constantly to prevent lumps from forming. Then cook, stirring constantly, until the sauce thickly coats the back of the spoon, about 6 minutes. Season to taste with salt and pepper, remove from the heat, and keep hot.

When the stew is ready, if necessary, gently reheat the white sauce over medium-low heat until hot, being careful that it doesn't scorch. Add the hot sauce to the stew and stir until the stew is thick and creamy, about 2 minutes.

Remove and discard the bay leaf. Stir in the reserved broccoli and cook just until heated through. Serve immediately.

Serves 4

Chankonabe

Sumo Wrestler's Stew

This hearty stew belongs to the tradition known as **nabemono**, or one-pot dishes. For these communal meals, the cook makes the broth and cuts the meats and vegetables that go into the earthenware pot, or **nabe**, but the dish itself is cooked by the diners on a portable gas burner placed in the center of the dinner table. They select the foods they want from an array of platters, simmer them in the broth, and when they have finished eating them, they add noodles (or sometimes rice) to the broth, which they then eat in soup bowls. Dipping sauces are usually provided, too, with **ponzu**, a citrus sauce, and **goma dare**, a sesame sauce, popular choices. If you want to try this dish, but you don't have a gas burner, you can cook the stew on the stove top, transfer it to a large bowl, and serve it family style.

Chankonabe is just one of many regional variations on the **nabemono**. It is traditionally eaten by sumo wrestlers as a way to put on the massive amount of weight they need for their sport. Don't be afraid that you will turn into a sumo wrestler if you eat this stew, however. The wrestlers eat much bigger portions—so big that they typically take a nap immediately after they leave the table, which helps them pack on the pounds.

Ground chicken mixture for **Tsukune**
  (page 114), shaped into quarter-size balls
1½ pounds cod fillet, cut into 2-inch chunks; shrimp, peeled and deveined; and/or shucked oysters, in any combination
6 ounces thick-cut sliced bacon, cut into 2-inch pieces
4 boneless, skinless chicken thighs, visible fat removed and cut into bite-size pieces
1 package (14 ounces) medium tofu, cut into 1-inch cubes
½ head napa cabbage or green head cabbage, outer layer of leaves discarded, leaves separated, and large leaves halved
2 leeks, white part only, halved lengthwise if large and then cut on the diagonal into 1-inch-thick pieces
6 green onions, including tender green tops, cut into 2-inch lengths

4 to 6 fresh shiitake mushrooms, stems discarded and caps quartered, or white mushrooms, stem ends trimmed and caps quartered
Ponzu sauce (page 19)
Goma dare (page 19)

Broth
6 cups reduced-fat, low-sodium canned broth, or 3 cups each regular chicken broth and water
¼ cup sake
⅓ cup plus 1 tablespoon mirin
2 tablespoons ginger juice (see page 16)
1½ teaspoons crushed garlic
½ cup miso, preferably white

4 to 6 cups cooked **udon** noodles (1 cup per person) or 2 to 3 cups cooked rice (see **Gohan**, page 140) (½ cup per person)

continued

Ready the meatballs, seafood, bacon, chicken, tofu, cabbage, leeks, green onions, and mushrooms and arrange on platters. Place the platters near the stove if you are making the stew on the stove top, or on the table if you are using a portable gas burner. Place the *ponzu* sauce and *goma dare* in individual dipping bowls and put on the table at each place setting. Also provide each diner with chopsticks, a soup spoon (optional), and a soup bowl.

If you are making the stew on the stove top, first make the broth. In a Dutch oven or other large pot, combine the chicken broth, sake, mirin, ginger juice, and garlic and bring to a simmer over medium heat. To add the miso, spoon several spoonfuls of broth into a small bowl, add the miso, and stir until smooth. Gradually add the miso mixture to the broth, stirring to avoid lumps. Once the miso has been incorporated, be careful not to let the broth boil.

Next, cook the foods in batches. Add some of each of the ingredients to the broth, simmer gently until cooked, and then serve them, returning to the stove to start a new batch as each previous batch is eaten. The timing will vary for the foods, but keep mind that the vegetables and tofu will cook more quickly than the meatballs, seafood, and chicken. Keep the broth at a gentle, steady simmer the entire time. If the liquid gets low, add a little water and/or chicken broth (or water and regular broth) so that you will have enough liquid to heat the noodles or rice at the end. Don't be concerned that the broth will become too thin. The flavorful ingredients that you cook in the broth will continue to enrich it.

If you are using a tabletop burner, you can make the broth on the stove top and then transfer it to the *nabe*, or you can make it in the *nabe*, though it is easier to start it on the stove top. When the broth is at a gentle, steady simmer, the diners can begin cooking. Each diner uses his or her chopsticks to slip pieces of the foods into the broth to cook and then retrieves them when they are done. Again, if the liquid gets low, add a little water and/or chicken broth so that you will have enough liquid to heat the noodles or rice at the end.

When everyone has had their fill of stew, remove any solids still in the broth and add the noodles or rice. Allow to simmer until heated through and then ladle into the soup bowls and serve.

Serves 4 to 6

Iridori

Sweet Simmered Chicken and Vegetables

This dish was inspired by a **bento** I ate on a train ride in southern Honshu, Japan's main island. Shohei and I had left the kids with his parents and had taken an eight-hour train trip to see a part of Japan that he had never visited. It was interesting to pass all of the small towns and villages as we sped or crawled, depending on whether we were on a local or a bullet train, through the countryside. At one of the larger stations, we found a terrific array of **bento** boxes to choose from, and we nearly missed the train as I agonized over which one to try. I picked a lunch box that held sweet-and-savory ground chicken and vegetables—a great choice—and I spent the next couple of hours trying to figure out exactly what was in it so I could re-create it at home. I think I got pretty close. You can serve this dish hot with rice, or at room temperature, also with rice, in a **bento**.

½ cup trimmed, cut up green beans
  (2-inch pieces)
5 tablespoons mirin
5 tablespoons sake
3 tablespoons soy sauce
2 tablespoons sugar
1 tablespoon canola or other neutral oil
1 tablespoon sesame oil
½ pound ground chicken
4 fresh shiitake mushrooms, stems discarded
  and caps quartered

½ cup sliced bamboo shoots
1 carrot, peeled, halved lengthwise,
  and then cut crosswise into ¼-inch-thick
  half-moons
1 parsnip, peeled, halved lengthwise,
  and then cut crosswise into ¼-inch-thick
  half-moons
Salt

Bring a small saucepan filled with water to a boil, add the green beans, and blanch for 1 minute. Drain into a sieve and immediately hold under running cold water to halt the cooking. Place near the stove. In a small bowl, stir together the mirin, sake, soy sauce, and sugar until the sugar dissolves. Place the bowl near the stove.

In a large frying pan, heat the canola and sesame oils over medium-high heat. When they are hot, swirl to coat the bottom and sides of the pan and add the chicken, breaking it up with a spatula. Cook, stirring, until half cooked, about 3 minutes. Add the mushrooms, bamboo shoots, carrot, and parsnip and cook, stirring, until the chicken is cooked through and the vegetables have started to soften, 5 to 7 minutes. Add the mirin mixture, mix well, and reduce the heat to medium. Continue to cook, stirring occasionally, until the vegetables are tender, about 5 minutes longer.

Season to taste with salt, add the green beans, stir to mix, and heat through. Transfer to a serving bowl or platter and serve.

Serves 2

Toriniku Kara-age

Fried Marinated Chicken

This is Japan's national fried chicken dish, a standard appetizer or main course for lunch or dinner and great with beer. I experimented with different marinades and flours to come up with this version, but as you get familiar with the basic recipe, you can customize to your taste by adding more garlic, ginger, or other spices, such as curry powder, to the marinade. Cornstarch makes for a very crispy chicken, but all-purpose flour is also an option. My husband is happy anytime I make this dish, and my three-year-old tries to beat everyone to the table so she will get a bigger share. I always make extra and set it aside out of sight to be eaten cold for lunch the next day. (For tips on deep-frying, see page 57.)

Marinade
1 cup soy sauce
1 small yellow onion, grated
2 teaspoons peeled and grated fresh ginger
2 teaspoons finely minced garlic

1 pound boneless, skinless chicken thighs
Canola or other neutral oil for deep-frying
1½ cups cornstarch
Lemon wedges

To make the marinade, in a bowl, combine the soy sauce, onion, ginger, and garlic and stir well.

Remove any visible fat from the chicken thighs and then cut on the diagonal into pieces about 1½ inches long and ½ to ¾ inch thick. (Cutting the pieces on the diagonal will ensure that they are not too thick, so they will cook more evenly.)

Add the chicken to the marinade and let stand at room temperature for at least 10 minutes but for no more than 30 minutes or the chicken will become tough.

Pour the oil to a depth of 3 inches into a wok or deep, wide pot and heat to 350°F on a deep-frying thermometer or until bubbles immediately form around a wooden chopstick held upright in the pan.

While the oil is heating, remove the chicken from the marinade and coat it with the cornstarch. (I do this by putting all the cornstarch in a large bowl and dropping the chicken pieces into it. You will probably need to fry the chicken in batches, so only drop as much chicken into the cornstarch as you can deep-fry at one time.)

When the oil is ready, remove the chicken from the cornstarch, shaking off the excess, and carefully drop the chicken into the hot oil. If the oil bubbles excessively or foams, reduce the heat slightly. Cook, turning frequently with chopsticks or tongs to ensure even cooking, until the chicken is very brown and crisp, about 6 minutes. Using the chopsticks or tongs, transfer the chicken to a wire rack or paper towels to drain. Repeat until all the chicken is cooked.

Serve the chicken hot with the lemon wedges for immediate gratification, but enjoy it any temperature afterward.

Serves 4

Tebasaki

Grilled Chicken Wings

Found at *yatai* (see page 115) and on *izakaya* (see page 30) menus, this dish calls for only the simplest of ingredients and techniques. It makes a great appetizer, and is also perfect for casual parties. When cooks use chicken wings for *yakitori*, they skewer small wings and sprinkle them with salt or baste them with a sweet sauce of soy and mirin. At my house, I use the largest, freshest chicken wings that I can find, salt them liberally, and grill them, without skewers, until they are crispy and smoky but still juicy. I can't wait to eat them, and burn my tongue every time!

10 to 12 large chicken wings (see note)
Salt

Shichimi togarashi (page 20; optional)

Pat the wings dry. Arrange the wings on a tray or platter and place in the refrigerator, uncovered, for 1 hour to dry further. This will produce a crispier skin.

Prepare a medium-hot fire in a charcoal grill, or preheat a gas grill to medium-high. Remove the wings from the refrigerator and salt them generously.

When the grill is ready, place the wings directly over the heat, cover the grill, and cook, checking and turning every 5 minutes or so, until crispy and browned on both sides, about 15 minutes.

Remove from the grill and serve piping hot. Sprinkle with the *shichimi togarashi*, if desired

Serves 4

Note: I leave the wing tips intact, though some cooks cut them off because they find the tips burn easily. That hasn't been a problem for me.

Toriniku no Leba Yakitori

Grilled Chicken Liver Skewers

If you like chicken livers, you will love these skewers. And if you are trying to convince someone how good liver can taste, this is a great recipe to serve. Grilling the livers imparts a smokiness and makes the outside slightly crisp, while the interior remains creamy. Be sure not to overcook them.

1 pound fresh or frozen chicken livers
Salt

Fresh livers are best, of course, but if you have purchased frozen ones, thaw them completely in the refrigerator. Rinse the livers and pat dry well with paper towels. Remove all visible yellow fat and any tendons. If the livers are large, you can cut them into 2 pieces, though it is not necessary.

Place 10 to 15 bamboo skewers in water to cover at least 30 minutes before grilling. Prepare a medium-hot fire in a charcoal grill, or preheat a gas grill to low.

Drain the skewers. Thread the livers onto the skewers, using about 4 pieces for each skewer. (The number you use for each skewer will depend on the size of the livers.) Sprinkle salt evenly over the livers. Place the skewers around the edges of a hot charcoal fire or directly over low heat on a gas grill and grill, turning once, until lightly browned on both sides. The livers will cook very fast, in only about 4 minutes, and can be a challenge to turn, so keep a watchful eye that you don't lose any to the fire. Alternatively, if you don't want to skewer the livers, you can cook them exactly as above but on a fish grill so they don't fall into the fire.

Remove the skewers from the grill and serve hot.

Makes 10 to 15 skewers

Tsukune

Grilled Ground Chicken Skewers

One of my favorite *yakitori* (see page 115), this same ground chicken mixture is used in *Chankonabe* (page 107) and *Toriniku Dango no Amasu An* (page 119) and can be used in place of the meatballs in *Kabu to Niku Dango* (page 98). Plus, I've shaped this tasty mixture into patties for teriyaki chicken "hamburgers," cooked on an outdoor grill or in a stove-top grill pan.

Basting Sauce
½ cup soy sauce
¼ cup mirin
2 tablespoons sugar

Ground Chicken Mixture
½ pound ground chicken
½ large egg (beat the whole egg, then divide in half)

2 teaspoons ginger juice (see page 16)
2 teaspoons soy sauce
1 tablespoon cornstarch
6 tablespoons **panko** (page 18)
3 tablespoons finely chopped green onion, including tender green tops

Canola or other neutral oil for brushing grill

Place 10 to 12 bamboo skewers in water to cover at least 30 minutes before grilling. Prepare a medium-hot fire in a charcoal grill, or preheat a gas grill to medium-high.

To make the sauce, in a small saucepan, combine the soy sauce, mirin, and sugar over medium-low heat and cook, stirring, until the sugar has dissolved and the liquid just begins to turn syrupy, 5 to 8 minutes. Remove from the heat and set aside in a small bowl.

To make the ground chicken mixture, in a large bowl, combine the chicken, egg, ginger juice, soy sauce, cornstarch, **panko**, and green onion. Using your hands, mix to distribute all the ingredients evenly.

Drain the skewers. Moisten your hands and, holding a skewer in one hand, grab a small palm-size clump of the chicken mixture and form it into a cylinder on the skewer, squeezing the mixture to pack it in place. The mixture is soft and can flop off if not shaped well, so the trick is to form a cylinder with a thickness of no more than $1/2$ inch at any point. As each cylinder is formed, carefully lay the skewer on a large plate.

The grilling goes quickly, so set up your workstation next to the grill before you begin: the plate holding the skewers, the bowl of sauce, a basting brush, and tongs for turning the skewers. Brush the grill grate lightly with oil and then place the skewers directly over the heat. Grill until the first side changes color and the meat mixture doesn't threaten to fall off the skewer when you turn it over, about 1 minute. Carefully turn the skewers over and cook the second side. (You may need to grab the meat gently, rather than the skewer, so that the meat stays in place.) While the side second is cooking, paint the top of each skewer with a generous amount of the sauce. Once the second side has changed color and the meat has set, after about 1 minute, turn the skewers again and paint the second side with the sauce. Repeat turning the skewers and painting with sauce 3 or 4 times, or until the chicken is cooked through. The total cooking time will be 5 to 7 minutes. If the sauce appears to be burning at any point, move the skewers to a cooler part of the grill, or reduce the heat if using a gas grill.

Remove the skewers from the grill and serve hot. They also taste good at room temperature or cold, sliced and served in a *bento* (boxed lunch) with rice and other items, such as potato croquettes (page 50) or potato or macaroni salad (page 72).

Makes about 10 skewers

Yakitori

Walking down the alleys near the business districts in Tokyo, or beneath the noisy elevated train tracks, you will find whole villages of casual outdoor eating and drinking places, some of them no more than pushcarts or stalls with a couple of stools. These street stands, or *yatai*, each specialize in a different preparation, from *oden*, a stewlike dish made with fish cake, and *yakisoba* (page 152), a delicious mix of noodles, vegetables, and meat fried on a griddle, to *yakitori*, grilled chicken skewers.

Stands offering *yakitori*, literally "burned chicken," give customers a wide array of choices, including thighs, wings, livers, hearts, and more. The skewers are basted with a sweet-and-savory soy-based glaze—the same sauce used for teriyaki—and are eaten simply, rarely with accompaniments other than a glass of beer and perhaps some *shichimi togarashi* (page 20) for sprinkling on the skewers. At home, you can serve the skewers as appetizers, or with a bowl of rice and a salad for a meal.

Toriniku to Negi Yakitori

Grilled Chicken and Onion Skewers

This simple recipe is good with salt (shio yakitori) or with sauce (tare yakitori). You can prepare half the recipe with the salt and half the recipe with the sauce to have the best of both worlds.

Basting Sauce (optional)
½ cup soy sauce
¼ cup mirin
2 tablespoons sugar

½ pound boneless, skinless chicken thighs, excess fat removed and cut into bite-size pieces

1 yellow onion, cut into 2-inch wedges, and/or baby leeks, white part only, cut into 1-inch lengths
1 tablespoon canola or other neutral oil
Salt (optional)

Place 10 to 12 bamboo skewers in water to cover at least 30 minutes before grilling. Prepare a medium-hot fire in a charcoal grill, or preheat a gas grill to medium-high.

If using the basting sauce, in a small saucepan, combine the soy sauce, mirin, and sugar over medium-low heat and cook, stirring, until the sugar has completely dissolved and the liquid just begins to turn syrupy, 5 to 8 minutes. Remove from the heat and set aside in a small bowl.

Drain the skewers. Thread the chicken pieces alternately with the onion pieces onto the skewers, using about 3 pieces of chicken and 2 pieces of onion for each skewer. As each skewer is ready, place on a plate. Brush the chicken and onion pieces lightly on all sides with the oil.

The grilling goes quickly, so set up your workstation next to the grill before you begin: the plate holding the skewers, the bowl of sauce and a basting brush and/or the salt, and tongs for turning the skewers. If using the basting sauce, either dip each skewer in the sauce or brush the sauce on the skewers and then place directly over the heat. Grill the skewers, turning 3 or 4 times and basting with additional sauce, until the chicken is cooked through and the onions are scorched around the edges, about 5 minutes total. If the sauce appears to be burning at any point, move the skewers to a cooler part of the grill, or reduce the heat if using a gas grill. If using salt instead of the basting sauce, place the skewers directly over the heat and grill, turning 3 or 4 times, until cooked through, about 5 minutes total. Sprinkle both sides of each skewer with salt and remove from the grill.

Serve the skewers piping hot.

Makes 10 to 12 skewers

Toriniku no Misoyaki

Chicken Grilled with Miso Glaze

Here is another great recipe for the grill. It can be cooked **yakitori** style (see page 115) by cutting the chicken into small pieces and threading them onto skewers. This same marinade can be used for beef strips, which can then be skewered and grilled with or without the miso glaze. Serve as a main course with rice and green salad or with potato or macaroni salad (page 72). Both the chicken, sliced, and the beef strips are also good in salads.

Marinade

1 tablespoon soy sauce
1/2 teaspoon sugar
1 tablespoon mirin
1 tablespoon sake
1/2 teaspoon peeled and grated fresh ginger

1 pound boneless, skinless chicken thighs,
    each cut in half and visible fat removed

Miso Glaze

1 tablespoon mirin
1 tablespoon sake
2 tablespoons sugar
1/4 cup miso, preferably white
3 tablespoons water

To make the marinade, in a shallow bowl large enough to accommodate the chicken thighs in a single layer, stir together the soy sauce, 1/2 teaspoon sugar, 1 tablespoon mirin, 1 tablespoon sake, and ginger. Add the chicken, turn to coat evenly, and let stand at room temperature for at least 15 minutes or for up to 2 hours in the refrigerator.

Prepare a medium fire in a charcoal grill, or preheat a gas grill to medium.

To make the miso glaze, in a small bowl, stir together the 1 tablespoon mirin, 1 tablespoon sake, 2 tablespoons sugar, miso, and water, mixing well. Set the bowl near the grill.

Remove the chicken from the marinade and discard the marinade. Place the chicken directly over the heat and grill for 5 minutes. Turn the chicken over, brush the top with some of the glaze, and grill for 5 minutes. Turn the chicken again and brush the second side with some of the glaze. Continue to grill, turning and brushing with the glaze every 5 minutes, until the chicken is cooked through, about 20 minutes total.

Remove the chicken from the grill and serve hot, warm, or at room temperature.

Serves 2 or 3

Toriniku Dango no Amasu An

Chicken Meatballs with Sweet Vinegar Glaze

Amasu literally means "sweet vinegar." These tasty little meatballs, made here with chicken, can also be made with ground pork or ground beef. Serve them as a main course with rice, a salad or other side dish, and Miso Shiru (page 44), or make them for your next party and serve them, speared with toothpicks, at room temperature as appetizers.

Ground chicken mixture for **Tsukune** (page 114)

Sauce
¼ cup reduced-fat, low-sodium canned chicken broth
¼ cup soy sauce

¼ cup rice vinegar
3 tablespoons sugar
1 tablespoon cornstarch
2 tablespoons water

2 tablespoons canola or other neutral oil

Mix the ground chicken mixture as directed for **Tsukune**. Moisten your hands and shape the mixture into 1-inch balls.

To make the sauce, in a small bowl, stir together the chicken broth, soy sauce, vinegar, and sugar until the sugar dissolves. Place near the stove. In another small bowl, stir together the cornstarch and water, mixing well, and place near the stove.

In a frying pan large enough to hold all the meatballs in a single layer, heat the oil over medium-high heat. When the oil is hot, add meatballs and cook, carefully shaking the pan to turn them so they cook evenly, until cooked through, about 5 minutes. Reduce the heat to medium and pour in the sauce. Continue to cook, shaking the pan to distribute the sauce evenly, until the sauce bubbles and the meatballs are evenly coated, about 3 minutes. (You may need to raise the heat slightly, but be careful that the sugar in the sauce does not burn.) Stir the water-cornstarch mixture to recombine and then pour it into the pan, distributing it evenly, and shake the pan again. The sauce will thicken slightly within 30 seconds to 1 minute.

Transfer the chicken balls and their sauce to a platter or individual plates and serve hot or at room temperature.

Serves 4 as a light main course or 8 as an appetizer

Gyudon

Sweet Simmered Beef and Onions over Rice

In the town near Tokyo where I lived, there was a small, counter-style restaurant directly across the street from the commuter train station. It had a sign that read 24 Hours Open and a picture of one dish and one dish only: the beef bowl. At the time I had a job that had me arriving home from work at about ten o'clock in the evening, by which point I was both starving and not much interested in cooking. I had no idea what "beef bowl" was, but I could read the price—cheap—and it certainly was quick and convenient. I had my first beef bowl, and like millions of other office workers, I was hooked.

Your choices are few: regular or omori (large), egg or no egg. The steaming beef-and-onion mixture is kept hot in a cauldron behind the counter. Rice is put in a large bowl, the beef and onion are ladled on top, and the bowl and an egg (if requested) are set in front of you. The customer mixes the raw egg into the bowl. The only sound in the restaurant is of rice and meat being shoveled directly from bowl into mouth. While the sauce recipe varies from restaurant chain to restaurant chain, this is my approximation of the sweet, winey, oniony late-night beef bowl.

2 tablespoons unsalted butter
1/2 large yellow onion, thinly sliced
1 tablespoon sake
1/3 cup plus 2 tablespoons white wine
1 1/4 cups water
3 tablespoons soy sauce
1/2 teaspoon ginger juice (see page 16)
2 tablespoons sugar

1/4 teaspoon very finely minced garlic
1/2 teaspoon salt
1/2 pound beef rib eye, very thinly sliced
   (almost shaved; for ease, freeze for 1 hour
   before slicing)
2 cups hot cooked rice (see **Gohan**,
   page 140)
2 large eggs (optional; see note)

In a medium saucepan, melt the butter over medium heat. When the butter is foaming, add the onion and cook, stirring often, until translucent, 4 to 5 minutes. Add the sake and wine and cook for about 2 minutes to cook off most of the alcohol. Add the water, soy sauce, ginger juice, sugar, garlic, and salt and mix well. Finally, add the beef and cook, stirring constantly to prevent the pieces from sticking together, until it is just cooked through. This beef should cook very quickly, in no more than 2 to 3 minutes.

Divide the rice between 2 bowls and spoon the beef-and-onion mixture over the top, also dividing evenly. Serve at once. If you like, provide each diner with an egg to mix into the hot beef and rice.

Serves 2

Note: There is a low rate of risk for exposure to salmonella bacteria in raw eggs. The elderly, the very young, pregnant women, and anyone who is ill or has a compromised immune system should not consume raw eggs.

Oneesan no Durai Kare

My Sister-in-law's Spicy Ground Beef and Vegetable Curry

Although I have no sisters of my own, I gained one through marriage, Mayumi, who is just a few months older than I am. Mayumi is the consummate Japanese housewife, caring for both her family of five and her elderly mother-in-law with tremendous efficiency and aplomb and never seeming to be overwhelmed by the tremendous amount of work she must handle. I have a lot of admiration for her: she works as hard and as smart as any career woman I know.

Mayumi has taught me a lot about real Japanese cooking. This dry curry is one of her standards because it is easy to pull together quickly from ingredients on hand, an important quality when you consider how busy Mayumi is. The recipe itself is so simple that her young daughter, Erika, is also able to pitch in and help cook it. Ground beef is usually used, but pork or even ground chicken will do if that is what you have, and you can substitute any number of vegetables for the ones included here. I like to use eggplant and English peas. You can top the dry curry with an egg fried sunny-side up for an authentic Japanese presentation.

2 tablespoons sake
3 tablespoons mirin
¼ cup water
¼ cup soy sauce
1 teaspoon salt
5 teaspoons curry powder
2 tablespoons unsalted butter
¾ pound ground beef
2 fresh shiitake mushrooms, stems discarded and caps minced

1 small carrot, peeled and finely chopped
1 yellow onion, minced
½ green bell pepper, seeded and minced
½ cup fresh or thawed, frozen corn kernels
1 teaspoon red pepper flakes
¼ teaspoon paprika
¼ apple, cored, peeled, and grated (optional)
3 to 4 cups hot cooked rice (see **Gohan**, page 140)

In a small bowl, combine the sake, mirin, water, soy sauce, salt, and curry powder and mix well. Set aside.

In a large frying pan or a wok, melt the butter over medium-high heat. When it is foaming, add the ground beef and cook, breaking it up with a spatula or spoon, until the meat has lost most of its redness, 3 to 4 minutes. Add the mushrooms, carrot, onion, bell pepper, corn, red pepper flakes, and paprika and cook, stirring constantly, until the onion, carrot, and bell pepper have softened, about 5 minutes. Add the sake mixture and the apple (if using) and cook, stirring constantly, until the liquid is absorbed or has evaporated, 3 to 4 minutes longer.

Transfer the curry to individual plates and spoon a mound of rice alongside. Serve piping hot.

Serves 4

Wafu Suteki

Japanese-Style Beef Steak

It is true that Japanese beef can be astronomically expensive. Nearly everyone has heard of Kobe beef, from cows that allegedly receive daily massages and sip beer to tenderize their meat, resulting in the priciest steaks in the world. But things have changed a lot in Japan over the years, and beef now usually turns up once a week, if not more frequently, in the average person's diet.

This simple steak is a common item on menus of yoshoku-ya (casual Western-style restaurants) and upscale coffee shops, and the plastic food models displayed in the windows of department-store restaurants in every big city reveal countless variations on steak: steak with a pat of butter, steak topped with grated daikon, steak topped with a fried egg, and more. Indeed, steak is never served plain; a sauce or topping is always involved, and many of these embellishments are familiar to the Western cook. The steak usually arrives at the table sizzling on a hot iron plate with a few baby carrots, maybe some snow peas, and with either panfried, French-fried, or steamed potato wedges on the side. This version is flavored with ginger and garlic, and is topped with grated radish and a little soy sauce.

4 sirloin steaks, each about ½ pound and 1 inch thick
4 tablespoons canola or other neutral oil
2 tablespoons sake

Sauce
3 tablespoons soy sauce
1 tablespoon peeled and grated fresh ginger
1 tablespoon sugar
2 tablespoons cornstarch

2 cloves garlic, crushed
1 cup grated daikon or red radishes (see page 15; you will need about 20 radishes)

Lay the steaks out on a cutting board, and tap them all over with the back of a heavy knife to tenderize them. Put the steaks in a shallow dish, pour in 2 tablespoons of the oil and the sake, and turn the steaks to coat evenly. Let stand at room temperature for 15 minutes.

To make the sauce, in a bowl, stir together the soy sauce, ginger, sugar, and cornstarch until the sugar and cornstarch dissolve. Add the sauce to the steaks and massage it into the meat.

Heat a large frying pan over medium-high heat. When the pan is hot, add the remaining 2 tablespoons oil and the garlic. When the oil is hot, remove the steaks from the dish, reserving the liquid in the dish, and place in the pan. (If you don't have a pan large enough, cook the steaks in 2 batches, using half of the oil and 1 garlic clove for each batch.) Cook, turning once, for about 4 minutes on each side for medium-rare. During the last minute of cooking, pour in the reserved liquid from the dish and boil to reduce slightly.

Transfer the steaks to individual plates, top each with ¼ cup of the grated daikon, and serve.

Serves 4

Hayashi Raisu

Beef and Onions in Tomato Gravy over Rice

This hearty, savory, beefy, tomatoey dish with a long *yoshoku* (Western-style; see page 8) history is commonly eaten at home in Japan, but it is generally made with the assistance of *hayashi raisu* sauce "cubes," sold in nearly every market. The dish is a staple of the Western-style coffee shop, too, where chefs slave over a demi-glace for days to create the complex-tasting sauce. I crave this dish, so I tried very hard to create a sauce in my home kitchen to match the taste of the real thing. I think you will find that without slaving for days (or even hours), you too can enjoy this popular dish. Shohei was happily surprised (and slightly shocked) when it turned up on our dinner table, and my version is now a family favorite. Serve it over a big bowl of rice or spoon it over *Omu Raisu* (page 39) instead of ketchup (a very hearty dish!). Any leftovers freeze nicely in zippered plastic freezer bags and are easily reheated in a microwave oven.

¾ pound beef rib eye, very thinly sliced (almost shaved; for ease, freeze for 1 hour before slicing)
½ teaspoon salt
½ teaspoon ground pepper
1 teaspoon plus 1 tablespoon sugar
3 tablespoons unsalted butter
1½ yellow onions, cut into ¼-inch-thick slices

½ cup sliced fresh white mushrooms
2½ tablespoons all-purpose flour
1 cup dry red wine
¾ cup tomato purée
3 tablespoons Worcestershire sauce
1 chicken or beef bouillon cube or ½ teaspoon granulated chicken stock base

Place the beef in a large bowl and sprinkle with the salt, pepper, and 1 teaspoon of the sugar. Using your hands, massage the seasonings evenly into the beef. Set aside.

In a large frying pan or a wok, melt 2 tablespoons of the butter over medium-high heat. When the butter is foaming, add the onions and cook, stirring often, until translucent and soft but not browned, 4 to 6 minutes. Transfer the onions to a Dutch oven or other heavy pot.

Add the remaining 1 tablespoon butter to the frying pan and return to medium-high heat. When the butter is foaming, add the meat and cook briefly, stirring constantly to prevent the pieces from sticking together. Add the mushrooms and, when the beef is almost cooked, after about 3 minutes, sprinkle in the flour and mix well. Add the wine, again stir well to combine with the beef and mushrooms, and then transfer to the pot holding the onions.

Place the pot over medium-high heat and heat until the mixture bubbles. Reduce the heat to medium-low, add the tomato purée, the remaining 1 tablespoon sugar, the Worcestershire sauce, and the bouillon cube and mix well. Cook, uncovered, for 15 minutes to blend the flavors.

Taste and adjust the seasoning with salt and pepper, then serve hot.

Serves 4

Kare Raisu

Curry Rice

A thick, mild or spicy classic based on English-style curry, **kare raisu** is arguably the best-known dish in Japan's large repertoire of "borrowed" cuisine. After its introduction in the late 1870s, curry rice became a hugely popular dish in universities and other schools, at lunch counters, and in homes. Tasty, cheap, and filling, it is still the meal of many college kids and office workers a couple of times a week.

Curry rice is sold at take-out shops everywhere, but even making it at home is a simple matter in Japan, where numerous brands of curry roux are sold. These flavor-packed cubes dissolve in water, instantly transforming it into a thick sauce, so that the cook only needs to add the beef and some vegetables, usually potatoes and carrots. Curry is also available with all the ingredients included in boil-in-the-bag, shelf-stable packets. There is even a boxed very mild, rather sweet version that my eighteen-month-old eats with gusto.

The thick, rich sauce is often served over **tonkatsu** (page 101) or **ebi furai** (page 78) with rice on the side. But it is most typically spooned over rice to soak up every last bit of flavor, and the dish is eaten with a spoon. Yogurt and grated apple are my secret flavorings for the curry.

3 tablespoons unsalted butter

5 tablespoons curry powder

2 large yellow onions, thinly sliced

1½ teaspoons minced garlic

1½ teaspoons peeled and minced fresh ginger

1 or 2 hot red chilies or 1 teaspoon red chili flakes

1 bay leaf

2 tablespoons all-purpose flour

1 pound boneless stewing beef, cut into 1-inch cubes

1 tablespoon canola or other neutral oil

1 tomato, halved, seeded, and chopped

2 cups reduced-fat, low-sodium canned chicken broth

2 small russet potatoes, peeled and cut into 1½-inch chunks

1 large carrot, peeled and cut into 1-inch chunks

1 teaspoon salt

2 tablespoons Worcestershire sauce

½ small apple, peeled, cored, and grated (optional)

2 tablespoons plain yogurt (optional)

4 to 5 cups hot cooked rice (see **Gohan**, page 140)

In a Dutch oven or other heavy pot, melt 2 tablespoons of the butter over medium-high heat. Add 2½ tablespoons of the curry powder and half of the onion slices, stir well, cover, and cook, uncovering and stirring every 2 minutes or so to prevent scorching, until the onions are medium brown, about 10 minutes. Uncover and stir in the garlic, ginger, chilies to taste, and bay leaf and stir to combine.

While the onions are cooking, spread the flour in a shallow bowl and lightly dust the beef cubes, shaking off any excess. In a large frying pan, heat the oil over medium-high heat. When the oil is hot, working in batches if necessary to avoid crowding, add the beef cubes and brown on all sides, 3 to 4 minutes. Transfer to a plate.

When the onion-curry mixture is ready, add the browned beef to the pot along with the tomato, mix well, and then pour in the broth. Bring to a simmer over medium heat and cook, uncovered, for 15 minutes.

Meanwhile, rinse the frying pan, return it to medium heat, and add the remaining 1 tablespoon butter. When the butter is foaming, add the potato and carrot chunks and cook, stirring, for about 2 minutes. Remove from the heat.

After the beef has cooked for 15 minutes, add the potato and carrot chunks, the remaining 2 1/2 tablespoons curry powder, the remaining onion slices, and the salt and stir well. Reduce the heat to medium-low, cover, and cook until the potatoes are soft but not disintegrating and the carrot and beef are tender, about 20 minutes longer.

Remove from the heat and stir in the Worcestershire sauce. Add the apple and/or yogurt (if using) and stir well. Divide the rice among 6 bowls and generously spoon the curry sauce over the top. Serve immediately.

Serves 6

Menchi Katsu

Crispy Minced Meat Patties

A juicy meat patty encased in a crispy **panko** coating and deep-fried is a guilty pleasure, but it is also one of Japan's most common lunch dishes, either slipped between bread slices spread with a little **tonkatsu** sauce for a sandwich or tucked into a **bento** (boxed lunch). I became hooked on **menchi katsu** one day while watching a food program on Japanese television in which chefs compete to create the most decadent, most delicious version of a popular Japanese dish. As they showed the chef preparing the **menchi katsu**, I couldn't help but wish that it was my dinner for the evening. The next day I went out and bought the ingredients to cook it myself.

The meat patty itself is similar to the Japanese **hamburg** (page 131), except that mayonnaise and brandy are added to help keep the meat juicy during deep-frying.

Meat Mixture
3 tablespoons **panko** (page 18)
¼ cup whole or low-fat milk
1 tablespoon unsalted butter
1 yellow onion, minced
¾ pound ground beef
½ pound ground pork
1 large egg, lightly beaten
2 tablespoons mayonnaise
1½ teaspoons minced garlic

Pinch of salt
¼ teaspoon ground pepper

1 cup all-purpose flour
1 large egg
2 to 3 cups **panko**
Canola or other neutral oil for deep-frying
Tonkatsu sauce (page 19)

To make the meat mixture, in a small bowl, mix together the 3 tablespoons **panko** and milk and set aside until needed. In a frying pan, melt the butter over medium heat. When the butter is foaming, add the onion and cook, stirring often, until translucent, 4 to 5 minutes. Remove from the heat and let cool.

In a large bowl, combine the beef, pork, cooled onion, **panko** mixture, the beaten egg, mayonnaise, garlic, salt, and pepper. Using your hands, mix to distribute all the ingredients evenly.

Spread the flour in a small, shallow bowl. Break the egg into a second shallow bowl and beat with chopsticks or a fork until well blended. Spread 2 cups of the **panko** in a third shallow bowl. Spread a little **panko** on a flat plate or tray.

Dampen your hands with water and form the meat mixture into round patties about 3 inches across and 1 inch thick. Gently dust each patty with the flour, shaking off the excess; coat with the egg; and then coat with the **panko**, lightly pressing the **panko** in place with your fingertips. As each patty is coated, set it aside on the **panko**-lined plate. As you work, add more **panko** to the bowl as needed. (At this point you can freeze the patties: arrange them on a platter or rimmed baking sheet, place in the freezer, and then transfer the frozen patties to a zippered plastic bag and return to the freezer for up to 3 months. You can deep-fry them directly from the freezer, but keep the oil temperature at 325° to 350°F. I usually start the cooking at 350°F and then lower it if the coating is cooking too fast. The patties will still be very crispy, but the crumb coating will look flatter than the coating on fried freshly made patties.)

Pour the oil to a depth of 3 inches into a wok or deep, wide saucepan and heat to 350°F on a deep-frying thermometer or until a bit of **panko** dropped into the hot oil rises immediately to the top. Working in batches, drop the patties into the oil one at a time, being careful not to crowd the pan, and fry, turning 2 or 3 times, until the **panko** is golden brown and the meat is cooked through, about 6 minutes. If the patties seem to be browning too quickly, reduce the heat slightly; they should be frying briskly but the oil should not be bubbling up too much. You may want to test a patty to determine the exact frying time. When they are ready, using tongs, remove the patties from the oil and drain on a wire rack or on paper towels.

Arrange the patties on individual plates and drizzle with the **tonkatsu** sauce. Serve hot. Alternatively, serve cold or at room temperature as a sandwich on untoasted white bread with a little **tonkatsu** sauce spread on it.

Serves 4

Hamburg

Japanese-Style Hamburger Steak with Sauce

Hamburg epitomizes the yoshoku concept—the perfect example of a Western dish adapted to Japanese taste. A popular home-cooked dish, it is a bit like meat loaf, but it is transformed by the rich sauce. My friend Ikuko and I made hamburg for our husbands one night, and it proved to be one of my first attempts at Japanese cooking to get Shohei's stamp of approval.

These patties are great served with steamed white rice, French fries, or boiled new potatoes and steamed and buttered carrots or green beans. The Japanese coffee shop touch is to serve it with an egg, fried sunny-side up, on top. I like to use a combination of beef and pork for texture and richness, but beef alone is also delicious. A similar blend of ingredients is formed into patties and deep-fried to make Menchi Katsu (page 128).

Hamburger steaks
1/3 cup **panko** (page 18)
1/4 cup whole or low-fat milk
3 tablespoons canola or other neutral oil
1 small yellow onion, minced
3/4 pound ground beef
1/4 pound ground pork

1 medium egg, lightly beaten
1/2 teaspoon salt
1/4 teaspoon ground pepper

2 tablespoons sake
1 cup **Hamburg So-su** (page 132)

To make the hamburger steaks, in a small bowl, mix together the panko and milk and set aside until needed. In a frying pan, heat 1 tablespoon of the oil over medium heat. When the oil is hot, add the onion and cook, stirring often, until lightly browned, 5 to 7 minutes. Remove from the heat and let cool completely.

In a large bowl, combine the beef, pork, panko mixture, cooled onion, egg, salt, and pepper. Using your hands, mix to distribute all the ingredients evenly. Gather the mixture into a large mass and slap it back into the bowl a few times. This action will help to create patties that are as dense as possible, with no interior air bubbles that might cause them to break apart during cooking. Divide the meat mixture into 4 equal portions. Form each portion into a patty about 1 1/2 inches thick.

In a frying pan large enough to accommodate the patties without crowding, heat the remaining 2 tablespoons oil over medium-high heat. (If you don't have a pan large enough, cook the patties in 2 batches, using half of the oil for each batch.) When the oil is hot, carefully add the patties and cook until a browned crust starts to form on the bottom, 4 to 5 minutes. Carefully turn the patties and cook until a browned crust starts to form on the second side, 4 to 5 minutes longer.

continued

Add 1 tablespoon of the sake to the pan, cover, and cook for 2 minutes. Uncover, carefully turn the patties over, add the remaining 1 tablespoon sake, re-cover, and cook until the patties are very brown on the outside and cooked through, about 2 minutes longer. As soon as the patties are done, uncover the pan, pour in the Hamburg So-su, and turn the patties once to coat both sides with the sauce. Cook for 1 to 2 minutes longer until the patties are well coated and the sauce is hot.

Remove from the heat and transfer to individual plates. Serve immediately.

Serves 4

Hamburg So-su (Hamburger Sauce): Here are two versions of the sauce. One relies on bottled tonkatsu sauce (see page 19) and one doesn't, so if you can't find the bottled sauce, you can still make this dish. Each version yields about 1 3/4 cups sauce. The leftover sauce can be stored in the refrigerator for up to 2 days and used on meatloaf or even as a sauce on an omelet. To make the sauce from scratch, in a small saucepan, combine 1 cup tomato ketchup, 1/4 cup Worcestershire sauce, 1/4 cup red wine, 1/4 cup water, and 1 teaspoon sugar and mix well. Cook over low to medium heat for about 3 minutes, then add to the hamburger patties and coat well. To make the sauce with bottled tonkatsu sauce, in a small saucepan, combine 1 cup tonkatsu sauce, 1/4 cup red wine, 1/4 cup water, and 2 tablespoons ketchup and mix well. Cook over low to medium heat for about 3 minutes.

Niku Jaga

Sweet Simmered Beef and Potatoes

The recipes for this favorite home-style meat-and-potato stew vary widely. Everyone's mother has a "secret" recipe, and the taste can be quite different from region to region and even house to house. This recipe combines my mother-in-law's version with a few embellishments to satisfy my family's tastes. Once you learn the basic recipe, you, too, can create your own variation. Some recipes include carrots, and others call for *shirataki*, thin, clear noodles made from a starchy root that have no taste of their own but readily soak up the flavor of the delicious broth. While there is no perfect substitute for *shirataki*, you can use rice noodles or bean threads (soak them first in hot water to reconstitute), both of which are sometimes found in regular markets, or you can skip the noodles altogether, as I have done here. You will also find small plates of *niku jaga* on *izakaya* (page 30) menus, and customers order it when they want a little bit of Japanese comfort food.

1 tablespoon canola or other neutral oil

½ pound beef sirloin, very thinly sliced (almost shaved; for ease, freeze for 1 hour before slicing)

3 large russet potatoes, peeled, cut into eighths, and immediately immersed in water to which 1 tablespoon rice vinegar or white vinegar has been added to prevent darkening

1 large yellow onion, thinly sliced

2½ cups water

3 tablespoons mirin

2 tablespoons sake

1½ tablespoons sugar

5 tablespoons soy sauce

10 to 20 snow peas, trimmed, blanched in boiling water for 1 minute, drained, immersed in ice water, and drained again

In a Dutch oven or other heavy pot, heat the oil over medium heat. When the oil is hot, add the beef and cook, stirring constantly to prevent the pieces from sticking, just until the color turns, about 2 minutes. Drain the potatoes, add to the pan with half of the onion slices, and then pour in the water. (The water should just cover the potatoes; if it doesn't, add a little more.) Bring to a simmer, cover, reduce the heat to medium-low, and cook until a skewer or chopstick inserted into a piece of potato goes in about ¼ inch easily, about 15 minutes.

Add the mirin, sake, sugar, soy sauce, and the rest of the onion slices, stir briefly to mix, cover with a drop-lid (see page 22), and cook over medium heat until the potatoes are cooked through, about 10 minutes longer.

Serve the stew hot in individual bowls and garnish with the snow peas.

Serves 4

Sukiyaki

Beef, Green Onions, and Vegetables in Sweet Soy Sauce

One of the best-known Japanese dishes in the West, sukiyaki gained popularity in Japan in the late 1800s, when the government started to promote beef after a centuries-long ban on eating it. This dish is a favorite of men (meat) and kids (sweet). I used to love to cook it at home in Japan because it takes only a little preparation, I could get it on the table fast, and it tastes good.

Japanese accompany sukiyaki with a small dish of beaten raw egg for dipping the sweet beef. In the United States, many people have an aversion to eating raw egg, either because they fear it might carry harmful bacteria or because they don't like the consistency. If you have a source for good, fresh eggs, you should give the egg a try, making sure you beat it well. The hot beef will cook the egg a little, the egg will cool down the meat a little, and the richness of the combined taste will be a pleasant surprise. Sukiyaki calls for **yakidofu**, "grilled tofu," which is available in packages at Japanese and Asian markets. However, it is easy to make yourself.

1 package (14 ounces) firm tofu

4½ tablespoons canola or other neutral oil

1 cup soy sauce

1 cup mirin

2 cups sake

3 to 4 tablespoons sugar

1 pound beef sirloin or any well-marbled beef, very thinly sliced (almost shaved; for ease, freeze for 1 hour before slicing)

3 leeks, white part only, cut on the diagonal into ½-inch-thick pieces

1 small yellow onion, halved through the stem end and cut into ¼-inch-thick slices

6 fresh shiitake mushrooms, stems discarded and caps halved

6 green onions, including tender green tops, cut on the diagonal into 2-inch pieces

½ head napa cabbage, cut into 1-inch squares

4 medium or large eggs (see note, page 120) or **ponzu** sauce (page 19)

Place the tofu block on several layers of paper towel on a large plate or cutting board. Top with several more layers of paper towel, and then place a plate on top. Finally, put a weight, such as a can of tomatoes or something similar, on top. Let drain for about 30 minutes, changing the paper towels (very carefully) once after 15 minutes. Remove the weight and the paper towels and pat the tofu dry.

Heat a ridged stove-top grill pan over high heat. When the pan is hot, add ½ tablespoon of the oil. When the oil is hot, add the tofu and cook, turning just once, until both sides have dark brown grill marks, 4 to 5 minutes on each side. Remove from the heat, let cool, and then cut into 1½-inch squares.

In a bowl, stir together the soy sauce, mirin, sake, and sugar until the sugar dissolves. (Use only 3 tablespoons of the sugar if you generally prefer your food not too sweet.) Set aside to use as the cooking sauce.

Heat a large nonstick frying pan over medium-high heat. When the pan is hot, add 1 tablespoon of the oil. When the oil is hot, add one-fourth of the meat and then one-fourth each of the tofu, leeks, yellow onion, mushrooms, green onions, and cabbage. Using a ladle, stir the sauce again to recombine (make sure the sugar has dissolved) and ladle a generous amount of sauce into the pan. The sauce should bubble a bit and the meat should cook very quickly. Everything should be ready in 5 to 6 minutes. The tofu will have become brown from the sauce, and the cabbage will become fairly soft, as will the onions and leeks. (This is normally prepared as a tabletop dish in Japan, so diners would remove the food from the pan themselves.) Transfer the contents of the pan to an individual bowl and repeat with the remaining ingredients and oil to make 3 more servings. It's best to serve each batch as it is cooked so it doesn't cool off, or, if you have an extra large "sukiyaki" pan, cook it all at once. (If you do this, reduce the oil to 2½ tablespoons.)

Serve each diner a bowl of beef, vegetables, and tofu. Provide small bowls, each with a well beaten egg or with a little ponʒu sauce, for dipping.

Serves 4

Rice, Noodles, and Dumplings

Rice is the most important food in the Japanese diet, and in Japan you see rice paddies nearly everywhere—even across the street from the supermarket in Shohei's hometown! Children are weaned on thin rice gruel, and a bowl of rice accompanies nearly every meal. **Donburi**, a bowl of hot rice topped with meat, fish, or vegetables, came about from the old tradition of pouring leftover soup over rice to make a meal and has evolved into a wildly popular one-dish meal. Indeed, rice is so central to the Japanese table that I usually keep some warm rice in the rice cooker or cook extra batches and freeze it so I can always put together a meal quickly.

Noodles are popular, too, and many types share a long history with rice in the archipelago. But others, including some of the best-known noodles in Japan today, originated elsewhere, among them the ubiquitous ramen, which was introduced by the Chinese. Japanese cooks have access to many, many different varieties of noodles, but in the United States, the choices are limited, so I have restricted the recipes in this chapter to the widely available ramen, soba, and **udon**.

Noodles are eaten for lunch, as an afternoon or late-night snack, or for dinner. In Japan, the range of presentations is dramatic. Office workers eat noodles **tachigui** style, at stand-up noodle shops, where you buy a ticket from a vending machine and your hot soba or **udon** noodle soup, **udon** topped with curry sauce, or other simple noodle dish is served to you in under three minutes—and consumed just as fast. Or, you can go to an elegant restaurant where the soba is hand-made and painstakingly styled for service on the finest hand-thrown ceramic tableware. At home, noodles are fried or served in a soup, in a **nabemono** (one-pot dish), or as a salad. Italian spaghetti is also popular, but prepared to please Japanese taste: with spicy codfish roe, with quick-boiled squid, with soy-based sauces, with a sprinkle of **yakinori** (page 18).

No matter what type of noodle you are eating, a strict etiquette is in force whenever you eat a noodle soup: you are encouraged to slurp the noodles, which ensures that you will enjoy them while they are still piping hot (as you slurp, you inhale air, which helps to cool off the noodles and thus avoid a burned mouth). However, use caution when you slurp. I have ruined many a nice shirt by splattering my noodles.

left: *Chirashi Zushi*, page 138

Chirashi Zushi

Home-Style Sushi over Rice

Mastering the art of creating traditional *nigiri* sushi (small pads of rice topped with raw fish) is best left to those who are willing to devote several years to intensive study and apprenticeship. Japanese eat sushi in restaurants or buy it from take-out establishments, but rarely make it at home. A few exceptions exist: *inari* sushi, fried tofu pouches that have been simmered in a mixture of sugar, mirin, and soy sauce and then stuffed with seasoned rice; *futomaki*, vegetables, egg, and *sushimeshi* (sushi rice) rolled in nori and cut into rounds; and *chirashi zushi*, sushi items scattered over a bowl of *sushimeshi*. The taste of the latter is similar to the sushi you eat in restaurants but is much easier to prepare. Your family will be impressed with both the presentation and the flavor. The idea is to make the dishes both look pretty and taste good.

Toppings

6 ounces raw shrimp; fresh-cooked crab-meat, picked over for shell fragments and cartilage; and/or **surimi** (imitation crabmeat)
2 tablespoons rice vinegar
2 teaspoons sugar
2 eggs
Salt
1 tablespoon canola or other neutral oil
2 ripe avocados, halved, pitted, peeled, cubed, and tossed with fresh lemon juice or rice vinegar to prevent darkening
2 ounces smoked salmon, cut into 2-inch wide strips (optional)
12 to 20 snow peas, trimmed, blanched in boiling water for 1 minute, drained, immersed in ice water, drained again, and slivered lengthwise

Mushrooms

2 cups water
2 tablespoons soy sauce
1 teaspoon mirin
1 tablespoon sake
2 tablespoons sugar
6 fresh shiitake mushrooms, stems discarded

Sushi Rice

¼ cup rice vinegar
2 tablespoons sugar
¾ teaspoon salt
3 cups hot cooked rice (see **Gohan**, page 140)

Yakinori (page 18), shredded or torn into small pieces, for garnish
Sesame seeds, toasted (see page 20), for garnish
Soy sauce for serving

First, ready the toppings. If using the shrimp, bring a saucepan filled with salted water to a boil. Add the shrimp and cook until they turn pink and begin to curl, about 3 minutes. Drain and, when cool enough to handle, peel and devein. In a bowl, stir together the 2 tablespoons rice vinegar and 1 teaspoon of the sugar until the sugar dissolves. Add the shrimp and let marinate for up to 1 hour. If using the crabmeat and/or **surimi**, marinate in the vinegar mixture as well.

In a bowl, beat the eggs with a fork or chopsticks until well blended. Add the remaining 1 teaspoon sugar and a pinch of salt and stir until the sugar dissolves. In a 10-inch nonstick frying pan, heat the oil over medium-high heat. When the oil is hot, pour in the egg mixture and swirl to cover the bottom of the pan. Cook, gently lifting the edges to let the uncooked egg flow underneath, until the bottom is set but not browned and the top is relatively dry, 4 to 5 minutes. Carefully slide the eggs out of the pan onto a flat plate and blot dry with a paper towel. Let cool and then cut into fine shreds (this is called kinshi tamago, or shredded omelet topping). Set aside. Ready the avocados, salmon (if using), and snow peas and set aside.

To prepare the mushrooms, in a small saucepan, combine the water, soy sauce, mirin, sake, and 2 tablespoons sugar and place over medium-low heat. Bring to a gentle simmer, stirring to dissolve the sugar. Add the mushrooms and cook until the sauce is greatly reduced and the mushrooms are thoroughly flavored, 15 to 20 minutes. (The timing isn't critical; just make sure that the mushrooms do not burn.) Remove the pan from the heat and let the mushrooms cool completely in the liquid, then remove the mushrooms from the liquid and slice them. Set aside.

Meanwhile, to make the sushi rice, in a small saucepan, combine the ¼ cup rice vinegar, 2 tablespoons sugar, and ¾ teaspoon salt over low heat and stir until the sugar and salt dissolve. Remove from the heat.

Place the hot rice in a large plastic or wooden tub or shallow bowl, spreading it evenly. Sprinkle the warm vinegar mixture evenly over the hot rice and, using a wooden rice spatula or wooden spoon, mix in the vinegar, repeatedly "cutting" down into the rice and turning it over to season it evenly. Continue mixing until the vinegar mixture is well combined with the rice, then let the rice cool to room temperature.

Mix the mushroom slices into the cooled rice, distributing them evenly, and divide the rice among 4 bowls. Using your own creative design, top each bowl with an equal amount of the shrimp and/or crabmeat, omelet shreds, smoked salmon (if using), avocado, and snow peas. Garnish with the yakinori and sesame seeds. (Never refrigerate the assembled bowls or the rice will become hard.)

Serve the sushi at room temperature. Provide each diner with a small dipping bowl for soy sauce for dipping the seafood or other ingredients.

Serves 4

Note: Japanese markets carry bottled seasoned rice vinegar for sushi rice. If you have some on hand, use ¼ cup of it in place of the vinegar mixture.

Photo on page 136

Gohan

Steamed Rice

Nearly every kitchen in Japan has a rice cooker. Indeed, cooking rice there is nearly unthinkable without one. They are amazing devices, sensing everything from the type of rice to its moisture content to its age. The machine uses "fuzzy logic" technology to cook perfect grains every time. Japanese are very particular about their rice, to the point that my husband tells me that he can taste the difference between the excellent California-grown rice we eat in San Francisco and the rice grown in Japan. (I thought I tasted a difference, too, until I realized I was probably just putting too much water in the rice cooker!) To cook rice using your rice cooker, follow the instructions that come with it and be sure to use the measuring cup provided for the rice (it does not relate to a regular cup measure.)

My mother in-law always has some warm rice in her rice cooker—she cooks five or six cups at a time—and she has freshly cooked rice ready for breakfast thanks to a timer on her machine that allows her a few more precious minutes of sleep in the morning. But not everyone has one of these handy appliances, so here is a stove-top method for cooking rice. If you keep a close eye on the pan, the rice will turn out fine. Here, I have cooked 1 cup raw rice, but you can cook more using the same formula of always adding about $1/4$ cup more water than rice. So, if you are cooking 2 cups raw rice, you will need $2 1/4$ cups water. Another way to measure the liquid is to put the washed rice in the saucepan and add water to cover by $1/2$ inch. The success of this method depends in part on not using a pan that is too lightweight. If your pan is thin, you will probably need to add a little more water.

To make 2 cups of cooked rice	To make 3 cups of cooked rice
1 cup short-grain white rice	1½ cups short-grain white rice
1¼ cups water	1¾ cups of water

In a heavy saucepan, rinse the rice well, massaging it with your hands and pouring off the cloudy water and adding fresh water until the water is nearly clear. Drain off the water well after the final rinsing.

Add the measured water to the pan, place over high heat, cover the pan tightly, and bring to a boil. Inside the pot (remember, no peeking) the rice water will begin to foam, which will be evidenced by the jumpy movements of the pan's lid. When this happens, reduce the heat to low, and cook until the liquid is completely absorbed, about 15 minutes (it is helpful to have a pan with a see-through lid). Remove from the heat and leave the rice in the pan, covered, for another 15 minutes. For rice with good texture, it is important not to remove the cover for this second 15 minutes.

With a wooden rice paddle or spoon, fluff the rice, and serve.

Sushi

Who hasn't heard of sushi? The term embraces a wide range of preparations that typically combine vinegared rice with fresh raw fish, shellfish, or fish roe. Some cooked and preserved items are used as well, such as boiled octopus, sweet egg omelet, vinegared mackerel, and more. Sushi, as I have already noted, is best enjoyed at restaurants or bought from take-out shops that specialize in its preparation, rather than made at home. Here are the basic types you will encounter:

Battera Rice and usually vinegared fish pressed in a mold

Chirashi zushi Fish, vegetables, and other items scattered over rice

Gunkan An oval of rice surrounded by a band of nori, with the filling (sea urchin, salmon roe, and so on) on top of the rice "fenced in" by the nori

Hosomaki Long, thin roll of rice encased in nori and filled with fish or vegetables

Nigiri Cylindrical pads of rice crowned with a tane (topping) of fish or shellfish, usually raw, or sweet egg omelet

Temaki Rice and a filling in a nori "cone" that is eaten out of hand

The Importance of Washing Rice

In the old days, before the advent of the rice cooker with its wonderful timer, Japanese housewives had to get up as early as farmers to start preparing the rice for the day. Washing the grains was one of the first tasks my mother-in-law entrusted me with in the kitchen, and as with so many things in Japan, there is a proper way to do it: The rice must be massaged vigorously under running cold water for a good four to five minutes (in the past, my "by-the-book" husband would always check to see if I had massaged it long enough). The idea is to release the starch, or talcum, that coats the kernels, thus ensuring that the cooked rice will have the correct stickiness and a clean taste. And don't toss away the cloudy washing water. It is touted to have myriad benefits, including a role in skin care: My mother-in-law sometimes saves it for washing her face. She's over sixty, with beautiful skin, so you can draw your own conclusions!

Onigiri

Rice Balls with Salmon Filling

Before running to my job in Tokyo, I liked to stop at a little stand near the office where an elderly woman sold nothing but rice balls. As soon as the last rice ball was sold each morning, she closed the stand. Onigiri is a quintessential Japanese food: a ball of rice, lightly salted on the outside and with a small treat, such as a pickled plum, flaked salmon, or sometimes even tuna with mayonnaise, inside. It is made by moms all over the country for breakfast, lunch boxes, and picnics, and it is the perfect handheld food (the nori wrapper keeps the sticky rice from getting all over your hand).

Onigiri can be made in any size, with less nori or more, according to your taste. If you make the balls but intend to eat them a few hours later, there is no need to refrigerate them. The nori, however, will no longer be crisp.

1 teaspoon salt
1 cup water
1 cup warm cooked rice (see **Gohan**, page 140)

4 teaspoons cooked and flaked fresh salmon
    or flaked canned salmon
2 sheets **yakinori** (page 18), each cut
    in half

In a shallow bowl, dissolve the salt in the water. Dip your hands into the salted water and grab $1/4$ cup of the rice. Using your hands, shape the rice into a small, fat triangle, and then use your thumb to create an indentation in the center of the rice triangle. Place a teaspoon of the salmon in the hollow, dampen your hands lightly again, and pat the rice over the hollow to encase the salmon. Create 3 more rice balls in the same manner.

Dry your hands thoroughly. Then, with the pointed end of the triangle facing the ceiling, wrap the nori around the bottom of each triangle, leaving the point showing between the two open ends of the nori. Eat immediately, or pack in your lunchbox for later.

Serves 2

Yaki Onigiri (Grilled Rice Balls) Variation: These rice balls have no filling and no nori. Instead, they are brushed with soy or miso and broiled until they are crispy and chewy on the outside and soft on the inside. Preheat the broiler (or you can use a toaster oven or an outdoor grill). Form the rice into fat triangles as directed. Place the rice balls on a rimmed baking sheet and slip into the broiler about 4 inches from the heat source. Broil the triangles, turning once, until they just start to brown on both sides. The timing will vary depending on your broiler. Remove from the broiler, evenly drizzle both sides of each triangle with 1 teaspoon soy sauce or brush with 1 teaspoon white miso, and return to the broiler. Broil, turning once, until both sides are very browned. Do not allow them to burn; especially watch the miso, which can burn quickly. These onigiri are delicious hot. You can also let them cool completely, freeze them, and reheat them in a microwave, finishing them under a broiler, until piping hot.

Oyako Donburi

Chicken and Egg Rice Bowl

Oyako literally means "parent and child"—the chicken and the egg—and this homey dish, in which pieces of tender chicken, soft scrambled eggs, and onions in a sweet soy-and-mirin sauce are served over rice, is a key recipe in every housewife's repertoire. My Japanese family and my American family like it equally. The sweet, oniony sauce soaks into the soft rice, which you can eat with a spoon. Some popular variations include substituting deep-fried chicken or pork cutlet (see **katsudon**; page 102) or thinly sliced beef for the chicken.

Oyako donburi, or oyakodon for short, is most often cooked in individual portions in a small frying pan, but for convenience, two portions can be cooked at once. It cooks quickly, so even if you are serving several people, no one will have to wait very long to eat. The eggs are just barely cooked, which adds to the overall pleasing soft texture of the dish. If you do not like soft-cooked eggs, you can increase the cooking time with the pan covered, but don't let the eggs get too hard.

2 small boneless, skinless chicken thighs
½ yellow onion, thinly sliced
4 large eggs
1½ cups hot cooked rice (see **Gohan**, page 140)

Sauce
1 tablespoon sake
3 tablespoons soy sauce
2 tablespoons mirin
1½ tablespoons sugar
1 cup reduced-fat, low-sodium canned chicken broth

Cut the chicken into bite-size pieces, trimming away any excess fat. Set aside. Have the onion, eggs, and rice ready.

To make the sauce, in a small frying pan, combine the sake, soy sauce, mirin, sugar, and chicken broth and bring to a brisk simmer over medium-high heat. Add the chicken and simmer until the chicken is about half cooked, about 5 minutes. Add the onion and cook until the chicken is cooked through and onion is soft, about 5 minutes longer.

While the chicken is cooking, break the eggs into a bowl and beat with a fork or chopsticks until well blended. Place about ³/₄ cup of the rice in each of 2 wide, shallow bowls.

When the chicken is ready, add three-fourths of the beaten egg to the chicken and onion and cover the pan. When the egg has just set, after 4 to 5 minutes, uncover, pour in the rest of the egg, and then immediately pour the chicken, onion, and egg mixture over the bowls of rice, dividing it evenly.

Serve immediately. Eat with chopsticks, and use a spoon to get every last bit of rice and sauce.

Serves 2

Chahan

Japanese-Style Fried Rice

Popular in homes and at lunch counters, this is one of the menu items that is best left to my husband to cook, whose fried rice always seems to turn out better than mine. It is a perfect way to use up leftovers and it is often the centerpiece of a family meal, accompanied by Gyoza (page 157), kara-age (page 110), or miso soup (page 44). Ramen restaurants traditionally offer a teishoku (daily special) of a bowl of ramen with the house-special chahan on the side.

To ensure success, get the pan really, really hot, put the beaten eggs in the pan first, and then put the rice on top of the eggs so that the rice doesn't get soggy. Finally, to make sure the rice kernels don't become too soft, use cold rice directly from the refrigerator and don't cook the dish too long. Here is the recipe for the Kaneko house-special chahan.

6 slices thick-cut or regular bacon, cut into 1-inch pieces
1 tablespoon sesame oil
1 tablespoon canola or other neutral oil
2 large eggs, lightly beaten
½ medium yellow onion, minced
5 green onions, including tender green tops, minced

3 cups cooked rice, preferably day-old rice cold from the refrigerator
1 chicken bouillon cube, crushed to a powder
1 tablespoon oyster sauce
¼ cup frozen English peas
¼ cup frozen corn kernels
Salt
Ground pepper

In a frying pan, fry the bacon over medium-high heat until some of the fat starts to render but the bacon does not start to crisp, about 4 minutes. Using a slotted spoon, transfer the bacon to paper towels to drain. Discard the bacon fat.

Heat a wok or the large frying pan over high heat. When the pan is smoking hot, add the sesame and canola oils and swirl the pan to coat the bottom and sides with the oils. Immediately add the eggs and, using a ladle, stir the eggs around in the pan, swirling and moving them until they begin to solidify, about 30 seconds. Add the yellow onion and cook for 1 minute longer, continuing to use the ladle to swirl the mixture around in the pan. Mix in the green onions. Next, add all of the rice, placing it on top of the egg mixture. Use the back of the ladle to press the rice into the egg mixture and to break up any lumps in the rice. Cook, continuing to press the lumps out of the rice, until all the lumps are gone and the eggs and onions are well integrated, about 2 minutes. Add the bouillon powder and oyster sauce and continue to press the rice and mix well. Add the peas and corn and mix well. (They will thaw as you cook.) Add the reserved bacon. Then, if you have the confidence, flip the rice by holding the handle of the pan and jerking it toward you repeatedly for about 1 minute. Otherwise, use a large spatula to move the rice around. Season to taste with salt and pepper. Turn out onto a platter or into a large bowl and serve steaming hot.

Serves 4

Hiyashi Chuka

Cold Noodle Salad with Sesame-and-Vinegar Sauce

As soon as the first breath of the warm, humid air typical of Japanese summers begins to stir, restaurants start serving this refreshing cold noodle salad with its tangy sauce. The warm weather alternative to hot ramen noodle soup, hiyashi chuka is a lunchtime favorite for office workers and a quick and cooling dinner for families. Packaged noodles and sauce make this salad a breeze to prepare in Japan—all the cook does is add the toppings. Even though in the United States I have to make the sauce from scratch, the dish is still very quick.

At our house, we like to experiment with the toppings. Shredded omelet, julienned cucumber, cold roast pork (chashu), green onions, nori, and sometimes tomato wedges are typical, but any chilled seafood, ham, snow peas, sliced radishes, or julienned carrots are also good additions. Traditionally, yellow wheat noodles, typically labeled hiyashi chuka or ramen in Japanese markets, are used, and they can occasionally be found fresh, stocked with the refrigerated tofu in regular supermarkets. If you can find them, use them, boiling them until al dente and then cooling them in ice-cold water. When I can't find hiyashi chuka noodles or fresh ramen noodles, I end up using spaghetti, which is a reasonable substitute, even though Shohei doesn't think so.

½ pound fresh ramen noodles or spaghetti
2 large eggs
½ teaspoon sugar
Pinch of salt
1 tablespoon canola or other neutral oil
¼ pound small or medium shrimp
4 slices ham (any kind), about 2 ounces total weight, cut into narrow strips
1 English cucumber, peeled, cut crosswise into 3-inch lengths, and then julienned
4 green onions, including tender green tops, minced
2 to 4 teaspoons **beni shoga** (page 16) (optional)
Yakinori (page 18), shredded

Sauce
¾ cup water
¼ cup sugar
½ cup soy sauce
¼ cup rice vinegar
2 tablespoons sesame seeds, toasted and ground (see page 20)
1 teaspoon sesame oil

Karashi (page 16)

Bring a large pot filled with water to a boil. Add the noodles and boil according to the package directions until al dente. Drain into a colander and immediately rinse thoroughly under cold running water until completely cool. Set aside.

While the noodles are cooking, prepare the toppings. In a bowl, beat the eggs with a fork or chopsticks until well blended. Add the $1/2$ teaspoon sugar and salt and stir until the sugar dissolves. In a 10-inch nonstick frying pan, heat the oil over medium-high heat. When the oil is hot, pour in the egg mixture and swirl to cover the bottom of the pan. Cook, gently lifting the edges to let the uncooked egg flow underneath, until the bottom is cooked but not browned and the top is relatively dry, 4 to 5 minutes. Carefully slide the eggs out of the pan onto a flat plate and blot dry with a paper towel. Let cool and then cut into fine shreds. Set aside.

Bring a saucepan filled with salted water to a boil. Add the shrimp and cook until they turn pink and begin to curl, about 3 minutes. Drain and, when cool enough to handle, peel and devein. Ready the ham, cucumber, green onions, beni shoga (if using), and yakinori and set aside with the shrimp.

To make the sauce, in a large bowl, stir together the water, $1/4$ cup sugar, soy sauce, vinegar, sesame seeds, and sesame oil until the sugar dissolves.

To assemble the salad, divide the noodles between 2 plates, piling them attractively. Top each pile with half of the omelet shreds, shrimp, ham, cucumber, and green onions. Pour half of the sauce over each plate (don't worry if it seems like too much sauce—you want there to be plenty). Garnish with the beni shoga and a little yakinori, and place a dab of karashi alongside each serving for the diner to mix into the noodles as desired.

Serves 2

Kurumi Soba

Cold Soba Noodles with Sweet Walnut Dipping Sauce

Soba noodles, which are made from buckwheat flour and have a firm texture and a slightly nutty flavor, are available in many different varieties in Japan. The most common type, which is a pale brown, is made with buckwheat and wheat flours, but some versions incorporate mountain yam, green tea, or other ingredients into the dough. Most of the soba noodles sold in the United States are made from a mix of buckwheat and wheat flours, and the most important thing to remember when boiling them is not to overcook them. They must never be mushy, especially when used in cold noodle dishes. In Japan, the water in which soba is cooked is thought to be full of vitamins and is thus drunk at the end of the meal, mixed with any leftover dipping sauce.

My husband is from Nagano, the heart of Japan's soba country. Shohei's whole family takes these noodles seriously. His hometown has many soba-ya (soba restaurants), including some where you can watch the noodles being made. (Making them is a laborious task, and though a lot of Japanese housewives try it as a badge of honor, they usually try it only once—myself included!). Every member of his family has a favorite soba-ya, and they argue every time about where to go to eat. Even now I have a favorite, Kusabue. I like the kurumi soba served there, cold noodles with a sweet dipping sauce enriched with walnut paste. This is a microregional dish, essentially unknown outside the area. The sweet and nutty dipping sauce (a mixture of tsuyu, walnuts, and sugar) is a perfect counterpoint to the cool soba. Here is the secret recipe.

Tsuyu
1¼ cups dashi or water
2 tablespoons soy sauce
2 tablespoons mirin

1 cup walnuts
2 to 3 teaspoons sugar
1 package (14 ounces) dried soba
Wasabi paste for serving (optional)
4 green onions, including tender green tops, minced

Bring a large saucepan filled with water to a boil. Fill a large bowl with ice water and set aside.

While the water is heating, make the tsuyu. In a small saucepan, warm the dashi over medium-low heat. Add the soy sauce and mirin, stir to mix, remove from the heat, and let cool.

Place the walnuts in a small, dry frying pan over medium-high heat and toast, shaking the pan as needed to prevent scorching, until the nuts are fragrant and have taken on a little color, about 2 minutes. Remove from the heat and let cool. Place the toasted walnuts in a zippered plastic bag and seal closed, forcing out the air as you do. Using a meat pounder or the bottom of a large can, crush the nuts until they are about the size of peas. Transfer the crushed nuts to a suribachi (see page 22) or a regular mortar and grind finely. (Don't worry if the finely

continued

ground walnuts create lumps in the suribachi. Walnuts have a lot of oil, which can cause this to happen.) Add 2 teaspoons of the sugar and grind the sugar into the walnuts. Taste and add more sugar if you prefer a little more sweetness. Add 1 to 3 tablespoons of the tsuyu and grind or mix until all the sugar is incorporated and you have a thick paste. Set aside.

When the water is at a rolling boil, add the soba noodles and cook according to package directions until just al dente. Drain the noodles in a large sieve and then immediately transfer them to the ice water. Using your hands, swish the noodles around in the ice water to cool them down quickly. When cool, drain well and transfer to a large bowl.

To finish the dipping sauce, put about 2 tablespoons (or more, to taste) of the walnut paste in a dipping bowl for each diner. Set out the remaining tsuyu, the wasabi (if using), and the green onions, and let the diners add these ingredients to taste to the walnut paste, adding the onions last. Let diners know that they need to stir well to mix the wasabi and walnut paste fully into the sauce.

To eat, diners pick up a mouthful of the soba in their chopsticks and drop it into the dipping sauce, and then use the chopsticks to eat the soba directly from the dipping sauce bowl. (Don't put too much soba into the dipping sauce at one time—just add the noodles bite by bite.)

Serves 2

Zaru Soba (Cold Soba Noodles with Dipping Sauce) Variation: Follow the directions for cooking, draining, and cooling the soba. Omit the walnut paste, and serve the cold soba with the dipping sauce flavored with only wasabi paste and green onions. To make tenzaru soba, serve Yasai to Ebi Tempura (page 70) alongside the noodles.

Hot Soba Variations
To make tempura soba, combine ½ cup soy sauce, ½ cup mirin, and 4 cups dashi or reduced-fat, low-sodium chicken broth in a saucepan to make the soup base and bring just to a boil. Follow the directions for cooking and draining (but not cooling) the soba and then divide between 2 large soup bowls. Ladle in the hot soup base and top with Yasai to Ebi Tempura (page 70).

To make tsukimi soba, make the soup base as directed and bring just to a boil. Follow the directions for cooking and draining (but not cooling) the soba and then divide between 2 large soup bowls. Ladle in the hot soup base. Crack an egg into each bowl. The hot broth will partially cook the eggs (see note page 120). Garnish with green onions.

To make toriniku soba, make the soup base as directed above and bring just to a boil. Slice 1 boneless, skinless chicken breast or thigh. Add the slices to the hot soup and simmer just until cooked through, about 5 minutes. Follow the directions for cooking and draining (but not cooling) the soba and then divide between 2 large soup bowls. Ladle in the hot soup base and chicken and garnish with green onions.

Yakisoba

Saucy Panfried Noodles with Pork and Vegetables

There is nothing more **natsukashii** (nostalgic) than the smell of **yakisoba** cooking at street stands and at festivals in Japan. When I lived in Tokyo, my home was near Yoyogi Park, and it seemed that every weekend in the summer some kind of festival was going on and **yakisoba** stands were up and running. Since the ingredients are so basic and the only cooking implements needed are a griddle and a spatula, **yakisoba** is found just about everywhere, from convenience stores to lunch counters, street stalls to dining tables.

The key ingredient, a bottled sauce with the strong flavor of soy and Worcestershire sauce, is what gives **yakisoba** its distinctive tang. I have made these panfried noodles with Worcestershire sauce alone when I could not find the proper prepared sauce, and while it wasn't exactly the taste, it worked for me. A.1. or another steak sauce could also stand in for the real thing. Bottled **yakisoba** sauce, although it is used just for this dish, is available online and keeps well, so if you like stir-fried noodles, you should track it down. Fresh **yakisoba** noodles, usually vacuum packed, are sold in some regular supermarkets. If you can't find them, you can use packaged fresh Chinese wheat noodles (usually labeled **chuka-men** in Japanese markets). Or, you can use dried noodles labeled **chuka soba**, which must be boiled for 3 minutes, rinsed in cold water, and drained before frying. You could also use cooked spaghetti or egg noodles, although I don't because my husband finds them too inauthentic. (But between you and me, I bet they would taste just fine.) And if you can't find the traditional garnishes of **aonori** and/or **beni shoga**, you can use shredded **yakinori** (page 18) and/or sliced green onions instead—or you can skip the garnishes altogether. The noodles will still be great.

6 slices thick-cut bacon

2 tablespoons canola or other neutral oil

½ carrot, peeled and sliced into thin strips about 2 inches long and ½ inch wide

½ head green cabbage, cut into 1-inch squares

½ yellow onion, sliced into ¼-inch-thick wedges

2 packages (14 ounces each) **yakisoba** noodles (see recipe introduction)

¼ cup water

About 2 tablespoons **yakisoba** sauce (page 20) or 1 to 2 tablespoons Worcestershire sauce

Salt

Ground pepper

Aonori (page 18) and/or **beni shoga** (page 14) for garnish (optional)

Lay the bacon slices between two or so layers of paper towel and microwave on high for 3 minutes. The bacon will not be completely cooked, but some of the fat will have been rendered and absorbed by the towels. Alternatively, cook the bacon in a frying pan over medium-high heat, turning as needed, for 4 to 5 minutes to achieve the same result. Cut the bacon into 2-inch pieces and set aside.

Heat a wok or large frying pan over high heat. When the pan is hot, add the oil and swirl the pan to coat the bottom and sides with oil. When the oil is hot, add the carrot, cabbage, and onion and stir-fry for about 2 minutes. Add the bacon and stir to combine. Add the noodles, stir-fry for 1 minute, and then add the water, cover the pan, and cook for 1 minute longer. Uncover and allow any remaining water to evaporate.

Add the sauce to taste and continue to stir-fry to combine the sauce with the noodles and vegetables, 1 to 2 minutes. Season to taste with salt and pepper and transfer to a platter. Garnish as desired and serve immediately.

Serves 4

Sandowichi

From the first time I saw Japanese *sandowichi*, I was captivated by them. In contrast to the overstuffed sandwiches common in the United States, Japanese sandwiches are slimmer, softer, and, for me, irresistible. A wide array of them is sold at convenience stores, in train stations, and in department-store food floors. The most obvious foreign influence is tea sandwiches, and the fillings are recognizable riffs on both Western tradition and uniquely Japanese taste. The sandwiches are typically cut on the diagonal into two or four triangles, so the customer can see the filling, and then wrapped in cellophane.

Among the offerings you might find are sliced hard-boiled egg, thinly sliced cucumber or tomato, and a lettuce leaf on mayonnaise-spread bread; a ham slice and a lettuce leaf on buttered or mayonnaise-spread bread; finely minced hard-boiled eggs mixed with mayonnaise (egg salad) and a ham slice on buttered bread; potato salad on buttered bread; potato *korokke* (page 50), *tonkatsu* (page 101), or *menchi katsu* (page 128) with *tonkatsu* sauce on plain bread; and codfish roe seasoned with hot chili on buttered bread. There are dessert *sandowichi*, too, such as sweetened cream cheese and strawberries, and toasted *sandowichi*. For the latter, which usually include cheese, the sandwiches are panfried in butter until golden brown.

Among the most popular open-faced sandwiches is the so-called pizza toast, a thick slice of white bread topped with tomato sauce, shredded cheese, and various other ingredients, depending on the maker. It is toasted in a broiler and usually eaten for breakfast.

Shohei no Butaniku to Goma Ramen

Shohei's Special Pork and Sesame Ramen Noodle Soup

Ramen-ya, restaurants specializing in the serving of ramen dishes, are found all over the country. Television programs dedicated to finding the best ramen shops, divulging the secrets of the tastiest ramen soup broths, and uncovering local specialties are avidly watched. In the comedy Tampopo, a popular 1986 film by director Juzo Itami, two characters struggle to establish the best ramen shop in Japan. Rent the movie if you want to work up an appetite for these ubiquitous noodles!

In southern Japan, where pigs are raised, the ramen broth is made from boiled pork bones. In Tokyo, cooks make a soy sauce–based broth, while in Osaka, the broth is salt based. In Sapporo, in northern Japan, a hearty miso-based broth is standard. Ramen cooked at home (usually by the man of the house) is as individualized as the person preparing it. My husband likes spicy meat and sesame seeds, while I like a chilled version with a vinegar-based sauce (see Hiyashi Chuka, page 146). Ramen is truly a Japanese national obsession. Once you eat it, you are likely to become obsessed too. I've used instant ramen noodles here, as they are readily available, but if you have access to fresh ramen, use them! Just boil them to al dente before adding the broth and toppings.

1 teaspoon sesame oil

½ pound ground pork

1 tablespoon chili bean paste

1 teaspoon finely minced garlic

2 packages (3 ½ ounces each) instant ramen

4 cups reduced-fat, low-sodium canned chicken broth

¼ cup sesame seeds, toasted and ground (see page 20)

Hot chili oil (optional)

2 green onions, including tender green tops, minced

4 slices bamboo shoot (optional)

¼ cup bean sprouts, both ends trimmed (optional)

1 hard-boiled egg, peeled and halved lengthwise (optional)

In a frying pan, heat the sesame oil over medium-high heat. When the oil is hot, add the pork, breaking it up with a wooden spatula or spoon. Then add the chili bean paste and the garlic and cook, stirring often, until the pork is cooked through and a little crispy, about 4 minutes. Remove from the heat and set aside.

Open the ramen packages, discard the flavor packets, and then cook the ramen noodles in boiling water as directed on the package. Meanwhile, in a saucepan, bring the chicken broth to a boil over high heat.

Just before the noodles are done, divide the ground sesame seeds between 2 large soup bowls and pour the hot chicken broth over them, dividing it evenly. Drain the noodles and add them to the soup bowls, dividing them evenly and swirling them so that they don't stick together.

continued

Drizzle in a little hot chili oil (if using), and then top each bowl with an equal amount of the pork, green onions, bamboo slices, bean sprouts, and half of the hard-boiled egg, if using. Serve immediately.

Serves 2

Miso Corn Bata Ramen (Miso-Flavored Ramen Noodle Soup with Corn and Butter) Variation: The primary differences between this ramen and Shohei's sesame ramen is the absence of pork and of a sesame flavor and the addition of miso to the broth and a pat of butter just before serving. Omit the sesame oil, ground pork, chili bean paste, garlic, sesame seeds, and chili oil. Cook the noodles as directed. While the noodles are cooking, bring the chicken broth to a gentle simmer. Scoop out a few spoonfuls of the hot broth into a small bowl, stir in 2 tablespoons or more white miso, and then slowly incorporate the diluted miso into the broth. Do not let the broth boil. Drain the noodles, divide them between 2 large soup bowls, and then pour in the broth, dividing it evenly. Top each bowl with 1/4 cup thawed, frozen corn kernels or drained canned corn; equal amounts of the green onions; the bamboo slices, the bean sprouts, and half of the hard-boiled egg (if using). Finish each bowl with a pat of unsalted butter. Serve immediately.

Gyoza

Panfried Dumplings

When Shohei and I were living in Tokyo, all I ever had to do to get out of cooking dinner was to ask, "How about the gyoza place?" It was the one thing I knew I could get him to agree to instantly. Tokyo's back alleys are filled with tiny little restaurants: the gyoza place was one of these. I couldn't ever find it on my own, and frankly, given the neighborhood of tiny bars hidden in small alleys, I probably wouldn't have gone there on my own anyway. But the cook made some of the best gyoza in town.

There is nothing tastier than a gyoza with a crispy bottom and a juicy filling, and if you like beer, these tasty dumplings and beer are natural mates. This is a basic recipe, but you can customize it by adding ingredients you like. Just be sure not to make the filling too wet. The dumplings are not difficult to make, but they are time-consuming to stuff and shape, so I recommend you make a whole lot (it is a great group activity!) and freeze them for a quick meal or appetizer.

Filling

½ pound napa or green head cabbage, shredded and then finely chopped and squeezed between paper towels to remove excess moisture

¾ pound ground pork

2 green onions, including tender green tops, minced

3 fresh shiitake mushrooms, stems discarded and caps minced

½ bunch fresh chives, minced

1 teaspoon peeled and grated fresh ginger

1 teaspoon minced garlic

1 tablespoon sesame oil

1 tablespoon sake

1 teaspoon soy sauce

About 50 round gyoza or other Asian dumpling wrappers, each about 3 inches in diameter (the thinnest ones you can find)

1 tablespoon canola or other neutral oil and 1 tablespoon sesame oil for cooking each batch

2 tablespoons water for cooking each batch

Dipping Sauce

Soy sauce

Rice vinegar

Hot chili oil

To make the filling, in a large bowl, combine the cabbage, pork, green onions, mushrooms, chives, ginger, garlic, sesame oil, sake, and soy sauce. Using your hands, mix together just until thoroughly combined. Avoid handling the filling too much.

Place the stack of wrappers on a work surface and keep covered with a clean, damp kitchen towel or paper towel to prevent them from drying out. Holding a wrapper on the palm of one hand, place about 1 teaspoon of the filling in the center of the wrapper. With a fingertip,

continued

swipe one-half of the edge of the wrapper with a little water, and then fold over the other edge to meet the dampened edge, enclosing the filling and pinching to seal securely. With your fingers, make 3 or 4 evenly spaced pleats along the sealed edge and place the dumpling, flat side down (the side opposite the pleats) on a sheet of waxed paper. Repeat until all the filling has been used up. (At this point you can freeze as many dumplings as you like: arrange them on a rimmed baking sheet, place in the freezer, and then transfer the frozen dumplings to a zippered plastic bag and return to the freezer for up to 1 month. Cook them directly from the freezer, allowing a few minutes longer cooking time when the pan is covered.)

To cook the dumplings, heat a frying pan over high heat. When the pan is hot, add the canola and sesame oils, swirl to coat the bottom of the pan with the oils, and allow them to heat. When a drop of water flicked into the pan sizzles instantly, arrange about 12 dumplings in the pan, lining them up neatly and placing them flat side down and pleated edge up. Cook undisturbed until the bottoms are lightly browned, about 3 minutes. Add the water, then immediately cover the pan, reduce the heat to medium-high, and cook for 5 minutes. Uncover and cook for a few minutes longer until all the water has evaporated and the dumplings are dark brown and a little crusty on the bottom.

To serve, slide a spatula under the dumplings, being careful not to tear the wrappers, and flip them browned-side up onto a large plate or platter, still lined up.

For the dipping sauce, set out containers of soy sauce, vinegar, and hot chili oil. Provide each diner with a small dipping bowl to assemble a dip to taste.

Makes about 48 dumplings

Acknowledgments

First and foremost I want to thank my husband, Shohei, for his discerning palate, his tolerance, and his contribution to my Japanese culinary expertise. I must thank him, too, for all the extra babysitting he had to do (for two rambunctious toddlers) while I was holed up working on this book. His input, taste testing, and parenting abilities were essential to the process. Thanks also to the Menjo family: Hiroshi san, Tomomi chan, and especially to Ekuko san (Ellie), who tested many of these recipes and gave them the benefit of her culinary experience. Ellie's professionalism and solid Japanese food preparation background made the recipe testing a lot easier, and Hiroshi's and Tomomi's bona fide Japanese tasting abilities (and ability to bridge the East and the West) helped make the book "the real thing" that I hoped it would be.

I want to thank the most supportive, encouraging editor ever, Bill LeBlond, and also Chronicle Books, for giving me the opportunity to share my passion and enthusiasm for Japan and for Japanese food. Thanks to Leslie Jonath, who shared the wealth of her enormous talent, for helping me sort out the trials and tribulations of writing. Thanks to Amy Treadwell for her careful work and forbearance, and to Aya Akazawa for her terrific art direction. Thanks to my best friend, the funny, fabulous, compassionate, and unwavering Andrea Burnett, and to Chris Navratil, for his encouragement and support. Without Sharon Silva editing this project, you wouldn't know a soba noodle from spaghetti—many, many thanks to Sharon for her careful work. My gratitude to Elizabeth Andoh, author, journalist, and founder of A Taste of Culture in Tokyo, for her wise advice and her willingness to help someone she hardly knew (and thanks to Patricia Unterman for introducing us). And thanks to my mom for understanding why I didn't have a lot of time to chat on the phone.

Finally, a heartfelt thank-you to the Kaneko and Ikegami families, especially Mayumi Ikegami, Emiko Kaneko, Noriko Shimada, and my mother in law, Miwako, for their unstinting help, advice, recipes, teaching, and, of course, for the kitchen slippers. I hope that your "foreign" relative has done a good job.

Sources

You will be able to cook most of the recipes in this book by shopping at a regular well-stocked supermarket. A few Japanese ingredients that are good to keep on hand are not as readily available, however. If you cannot find them in Japanese or other Asian markets where you live, these online suppliers will ship them to you.

ASIANFOODGROCER.COM
Carries a wide array of Japanese and other Asian foods, with pictures and descriptions to help you shop.

ASIAFOODS.COM
Stocks the basics, although the focus is not on Japanese foods.

ETHNICGROCER.COM
Carries some Japanese groceries, although not a large assortment.

EVERYTHINGCHOPSTICKS.COM
The name says it all.

KATAGIRI.COM
This is the online branch of the well-established New York Japanese market. Some familiarity with the ingredients is necessary to navigate it successfully, but it is well stocked with anything you would need to cook Japanese food, and it ships worldwide.

KOAMART.COM
This site is mostly for Korean food, but also carries a decent selection of Japanese food products along with kitchenware.

KROGER.COM
The Web site for the national supermarket chain has an extensive selection of "international" foods. For Japanese ingredients, click on the JFC store link and the Kikkoman store link. They are an especially easy source for prepared sauces.

MARUWA.COM
This address brings up the site in Japanese; click on the English button. You will find all Japanese groceries with photographs and descriptions.

MIDORIMART.COM
This site carries all the basic Japanese ingredients and kitchenware. Based in Philadelphia, Pennsylvania, delivery charges vary, based on distance.

MITSUWA MARKETPLACE
This large Japanese grocery store chain does not have a Web site, but it does have branches in northern New Jersey, Chicago, and in San Jose and several southern California communities.

MOUNTFUJI.CO.UK
A United Kingdom site that stocks all the basics for cooking Japanese food.

PACIFICRIMGOURMET.COM
This user-friendly site carries different types of Asian foods, including a good selection of Japanese items. It also has kitchenware and books.

Index

Table of Equivalents

The exact equivalents in the following tables have been rounded for convenience.

Liquid/Dry Measures

U.S.	METRIC
1/4 teaspoon	1.25 milliliters
1/2 teaspoon	2.5 milliliters
1 teaspoon	5 milliliters
1 tablespoon (3 teaspoons)	15 milliliters
1 fluid ounce (2 tablespoons)	30 milliliters
1/4 cup	60 milliliters
1/3 cup	80 milliliters
1/2 cup	120 milliliters
1 cup	240 milliliters
1 pint (2 cups)	480 milliliters
1 quart (4 cups, 32 ounces)	960 milliliters
1 gallon (4 quarts)	3.84 liters

U.S.	METRIC
1 ounce (by weight)	28 grams
1 pound	448 grams
2.2 pounds	1 kilogram

Oven Temperatures

FAHRENHEIT	CELSIUS	GAS
250	120	1/2
275	140	1
300	150	2
325	160	3
350	180	4
375	190	5
400	200	6
425	220	7
450	230	8
475	240	9
500	260	10

Lengths

U.S.	METRIC
1/3 inch	3 millimeters
1/4 inch	6 millimeters
1/2 inch	12 millimeters
1 inch	2.5 centimeters